AUSTRALIAN PLANTS FOR YEAR-ROUND COLOUR

GARDENING
AUSTRALIA

AUSTRALIAN PLANTS FOR YEAR-ROUND COLOUR

ANGUS STEWART

with photographs by Melinda Bargwanna

ABC
BOOKS

To my sister, Carolyn Stewart, a colourful character who has been an inspiration to me all my life.

Published by ABC Books for the
AUSTRALIAN BROADCASTING CORPORATION
GPO Box 9994 Sydney NSW 2001

Copyright © Australian Broadcasting Corporation 2002

First published September 2002

National Library of Australia
Cataloguing-in-Publication entry
Stewart, Angus
  Australian plants for year-round colour

  Includes index.
  ISBN 0 7333 0985 2

1. Wild flower gardening - Australia. 2. Native plant gardening - Australia.
3. Native plants for cultivation - Australia. I. Bargwanna, Melinda.
II. Australian Broadcasting Corporation. III. Title. (Series : Gardening Australia).

635.95194

Designed by Kerry Klinner
Set in Berkeley 11pt on 13pt leading
Colour reproduction by Pageset, Melbourne
Printed and bound in China by Everbest
5 4 3 2 1

Picture credits
Melinda Bargwanna
ii, iii, vi, 1, 4, 5, 8, 9, 12, 13, 16 (top), 17, 20, 24, 25 (bottom), 28 (top), 36, 37, 41 (bottom), 44, 45 (bottom right), 52 (top), 53, 56, 57 (bottom), 61, 65, 68, 69, 76 (top), 77, 80 (bottom), 81, 84, 85, 89 (top), 92, 93, 96 (bottom), 101, 104 (bottom), 105.

Angus Stewart
16 (bottom), 21, 25 (top), 28 (bottom), 29, 32, 33, 40, 41 (top), 45 (top and bottom left), 48, 49, 52 (bottom), 57 (top), 60, 64, 72, 73, 76 (bottom), 80 (top), 88, 89 (bottom), 96 (top), 97, 100, 104 (top).

Page ii Anigozanthos 'Regal Claw'
Page iii Flame pea (Chorizema cordatum)

Contents

Introduction

It is an exciting time for those gardeners who would like to use Australian plants in more creative ways in the garden. For many years native plants have been considered somewhat unfashionable. A boom in the use of Australian plants in the 1970s was followed by something of a backlash because many of the species used in that period were perhaps not totally appropriate for gardens or for the climatic zones where they were planted.

Some 30 years later, nurseries have become much more sophisticated in the selection and introduction of Australian plants for cultivation. Never before has there been such a wide choice of plant material available, in particular new cultivars (varieties) of native plants that have been selected for their improved performance in the garden. Many of the new types boast longer flowering periods and have a wider range of flower colours than was previously available.

The aim of this book is to show the reader how to create an Australian plant garden that will flower all year round. In

Above: New cultivars, such as Eucalyptus (synonym *Corymbia*) 'Summer Beauty' are much more reliable in cultivation than the parent species from which they were bred
Left: Through the use of grafting techniques, spectacular but often difficult to grow plants, such as the woolly feather flower (*Verticordia monodelpha*), are becoming more available to gardeners

large areas of Australia there is not a huge distinction between seasons and the plants have evolved to be evergreen, with flowering habits that are much less seasonal than those from climates such as Europe and the northern parts of the United States. Consequently, we have an excellent range of species that have extended periods of flowering throughout the year. It is, therefore, not too difficult to create an Australian plant garden that is truly colourful all year round.

We also look at the changing seasons and how different groups of Australian plants can be used to brighten each period of the year, and particularly those times such as winter when the garden can get a bit monotonous. In addition, this book gives helpful hints on how to promote better flowering in your Australian plants through specific maintenance techniques. Pruning is a vital part of this process, while watering and fertilising also play a critical role in building the best vegetative framework for spectacular and prolonged flowering. Other practices such as fertilising and mulching are also explored.

Finally, this book is very much about the plants themselves and it looks at the Australian plants which you can use to create a spectacular native garden that not only provides a kaleidoscope of colour through the seasons, but is also relatively easy to maintain and attracts abundant wildlife.

Designing with colour in the native garden

Colour plays a great part in influencing our moods. Using it, we can create excitement and energy with vibrant reds and yellows, or peace and serenity with blues and whites. Nature provides us with an endless palette of hues and tones to create whatever effect we fancy. The great beauty of colour in the garden is that it is an ever-changing feast for the senses through the seasons and through the years. By using annual plants, we can create different colour schemes at will.

In order to make the most of colour in your garden, it is useful to understand some of the basic principles involved. Colour is created when light is reflected from surfaces. A rainbow displays the full spectrum of colours visible to the human eye as it breaks down white light into its various component wavelengths. Short wavelengths give us the violet end of the spectrum, while long wavelengths take us to the red end of the spectrum.

The pigments contained in a surface absorb some wavelengths and reflect others. The wavelengths reflected give us the colour we see in that surface. The texture of a surface also influences reflection and therefore our perception of colour. A flower with a shiny texture, such as a waratah, reflects more light and will appear lighter in colour than a flower with a coarse, hairy texture such as a kangaroo paw.

Co-ordinating colour in the native garden

It is one thing to introduce a riot of colour into your garden; it is another thing to 'paint' with it in an artistic way. Designing with colour will really add an extra dimension to gardening for those people who enjoy creative endeavours with plants. To fully enhance your use of colour, it is worth thinking about a few of the principles of design. It should also be appreciated that colour in gardens is a transient thing that will change with the seasons, so do a little research on the plants you wish to introduce and you will be well rewarded.

It is always a temptation to go to nurseries and buy plants that are in flower on an impulse. This allows you to see the colour and form of the plant, but you should also try to keep to an overall plan in the garden that is based on the design principles outlined in the following sections.

The colour wheel

The colour wheel is an interesting concept that helps us to appreciate and best use colour qualities. It also shows the relationships between various colours. Colours adjacent to each other on the wheel are complementary, while those opposite each other on the wheel are contrasting. The primary colours are, of course, red, yellow and blue. The secondary colours are orange, green and violet, and these are created by mixing two primary colours in equal amounts. Finally, tertiary colours can be created by mixing primary and secondary colours. For example, mixing blue and green will create turquoise.

As a starting point, when designing your garden use colours adjacent to each other on the wheel to create harmonious effects, while combinations of opposite colours create dramatic eye-catching contrasts that

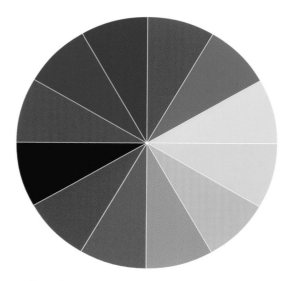

priority to the artistic side. In other words, the plants you use must also be suitable for your garden in a horticultural sense as well as from a colour design point of view.

To enjoy the greatest variety of Australian plants, the best planting spot is one with good drainage that receives full sun for most of the day. For the majority of flowering plants, the quantity of flowers they bear is proportional to the amount of sunlight they receive. There are, however, a number of plants that will flower well in shade, such as mint bushes, native violet and various rainforest species, and these provide many colour choices where conditions are not ideal.

make a bold statement. It is also worth considering that blues and violets create a 'cool' effect which is soothing and calming, while the red end of the spectrum provides 'warm' colours which create a livelier atmosphere.

Once you have decided what colours and combinations you would like from an artistic point of view, it is then a matter of choosing the plant material to make it happen. In this book, the chapter 'Plants A to Z' provides the plant palette with which to paint your colourful creation. However, it is also important to consider the horticultural practicalities of your design as an equal

Contrast and harmony

Australian plants can be used in many planting combinations that work particularly well both from a horticultural and a design point of view. These allow the gardener to choose a harmonious or a contrasting design effect to suit a particular part of the garden.

Harmonies

Mixing colours that are close together on the colour wheel will result in beautiful blends of colour that harmonise and this creates a garden that is less demanding on the eye. For example, the pastel shades of the

An example of a colour contrast that can be created is the yellow of various everlasting daisies and the blues of dampiera and *Lechenaultia biloba*

The soft pinks and whites of the rosy sunray (*Rhodanthe chlorocephala* subsp. *rosea*) create harmony in the garden

brachyscome daisies can be blended to create beautiful harmonies with pink- and white-flowering shrubs such as baeckeas, philothecas (eriostemons), boronias, and bottlebrushes (callistemons). Yellow and orange combinations, such as *Grevillea* 'Superb' with various acacias, also work extremely well.

Contrasts

Blue and orange is an incredibly striking combination. There are a number of exciting blue flowers in the Australian flora, such as dampiera and wahlenbergia. These can be coupled with the orange tones of grevilleas and kangaroo paws to create a magical effect. Contrasting blue with orange highlights the blue in a way that does not happen when it is blended with more complementary colours such as purple.

Red and green is another fantastic contrasting combination, such as when fiery red flowers are set against soothing green foliage. Some stunning examples are the New South Wales waratah, various bottlebrushes, and the New South Wales Christmas bush.

Yellow and purple, such as hibbertia and brachyscome planted with hardenbergia and mint bushes, creates a vibrant combination. This combination highlights yellow in a very vivid way, compared to combining yellow with a complementary colour such as orange which subdues the yellow effect. It very much depends what sort of effect you want. Another good combination is the purple fan flower (*Scaevola* species) with yellow everlasting daisies such as *Bracteantha* 'Dargan Hill Monarch'.

The moods of colour

Each colour of the spectrum imparts its own character to a garden and creates a mood, while combinations of colours will interact to create other interesting effects. Let's look at each colour in turn to see what it brings to the overall mix in the garden.

Yellow

Yellow is an extremely uplifting colour and the one to which the eye tends to be drawn first in any colour scheme. It is the closest colour to pure light, which of course is white, and this is perhaps why yellow is such an invigorating colour. Whichever shade of yellow is used, from lemon through to rich golden yellow, it will bring a cheerfulness to the garden and there are numerous examples of suitable plants within the Australian flora. It is worth considering some of the winter-flowering acacias such as Cootamundra wattle and Queensland silver wattle to bring bright light into the garden when there is not much other colour.

For a vibrant effect, shades of yellow can be combined using compatible plants. Try wattles (various *Acacia* species) and grevilleas such as 'Sandra Gordon' and creamy white 'Moonlight' for a taller layer of trees and shrubs; an intermediate layer of everlasting daisies (*Bracteantha bracteata*); and groundcovering plants including creepers such as the snake vine (*Hibbertia scandens*) and kangaroo paws such as the tough *Anigozanthos* 'Bush Gold'. The Western Australian cottonheads (*Conostylis* species) and some of the newer *Brachyscome* cultivars such as 'Sunburst' and 'Lemon Twist' can also be used to add yellow at ground level or in containers.

Lemon-scented myrtle (*Backhousia citriodora*) and trailing guinea flower (*Hibbertia dentata*) are plants from more moist rainforest-type conditions and should be considered for yellow colour in gardens in subtropical environments.

Also worth thinking about are plants with variegated foliage that feature yellow tones, such as variegated brush box (*Lophostemon confertus* 'Perth Gold'), *Agonis flexuosa* 'Variegata' and *Melaleuca bracteata* 'Revolution Gold'. The advantage of these plants is that colour is provided all year round; foliage colour is explored further on page 11.

Orange

This is a warm vibrant colour that also has a rather uplifting role in the garden. The lighter or pastel shades of orange are apricot and peach. They create a welcoming mood in the garden, while the darker shades of orange such as bronze are much more sombre and tend to work best with complementary colours such as yellows and reds. Peach imparts a softer effect on the colour scheme, particularly when mixed with silvery coloured plants such as flannel flower (*Actinotus helianthi*). The crimson kunzea (*Kunzea baxteri*) has very vibrant orange flowers cascading down among soft green foliage. Year-round orange flowers can be provided with shrubs such as *Grevillea* 'Superb' and *G.* 'Coconut Ice' or smaller plants such as kangaroo paws like *Anigozanthos* 'Bush Tango' and *A.* 'Bush Glow'.

Red

Red provides fiery excitement in the garden, however, be careful with it as too much of a good thing can lead to a hangover for the eye. It is not a restful colour but it does make for some interesting colour contrasts, particularly when used with its opposite on the colour wheel, green.

A hot colour scheme can be created using various reds. Trees such as the red-flowering gum (*Eucalyptus* syn. *Corymbia ficifolia*), the firewheel tree (*Stenocarpus sinuatus*) or the Illawarra flame tree (*Brachychiton acerifolius*) will provide an upper level of colour. The outstanding ever-blooming *Grevillea* 'Robyn Gordon' will provide a great shrubby backbone and can be complemented in spring with bold strokes from the New South Wales waratah (*Telopea speciosissima*), various bottlebrushes (*Callistemon* species and cultivars) and the crimson kunzea

(*Kunzea baxteri*). To finish the picture, lower-growing plants such as the groundcovering *Grevillea* 'Poorinda Royal Mantle', running postman (*Kennedia prostrata*) and the long-flowering kangaroo paw *Anigozanthos* 'Bush Ranger' can all be grown happily together.

Violet

Violet is a rather subdued, sombre colour in most garden situations. It makes a restful combination with blues, silvers and greys, but, if you combine it with bright yellow, the contrast can be very eye-catching. If you are looking for excitement, you could combine the beautiful violet-mauves of the native mint bushes (various *Prostanthera* species) with the bright yellow of some of the wattles. On the other hand, the blue-grey of some of the eucalypts such as *Eucalyptus cinerea* will create a more subdued scene. Various native daisies, such as *Brachyscome multifida* 'Break O' Day' or *B. angustifolia,* can be used to provide violet tones at ground level, along with the fan flowers such as *Scaevola* 'Purple Fanfare' or *S.* 'Mauve Clusters'.

Pink

Those preferring pastel pinks have some inspiring plants to choose from, including trees such as red ironbark (*Eucalyptus sideroxylon*) or the pink new foliage of *Callistemon salignus*. Shrubs such as *Grevillea* 'Misty Pink', *Callistemon* 'Candy Pink' or *C.* 'Perth Pink', pink rice flower (*Pimelea ferruginea*), and the long-flowering rock thryptomene (*Thryptomene saxicola*) will give colour at eye level, while a lower level can be filled with groundcovers such as *Brachyscome multifida* 'Pink Haze' and *Scaevola* 'Misty Pink' or even annuals such as rosy sunray (*Rhodanthe chlorocephala* subsp. *rosea*—formerly known and sold as *Helipterum roseum*).

Callistemon 'Kings Park Special'

The fruit of the spiny-headed matrush (*Lomandra longfolia*)

Pincushion hakea (*Hakea laurina*)

Green

This is a restful, gentle colour that abounds in the garden for obvious reasons. It is the colour of chlorophyll, which of course is the world's most important pigment! Apart from foliage, the Australian flora also contains some interesting green flowers such as the metallic green of the kangaroo paw *Anigozanthos viridis* or the light green of its taller cousin *A. flavidus*.

The classic glossy green leaves of the lillypillies (*Acmena* and *Syzygium* species) have become popular for their foliage alone as hedge and topiary plants. Many of their rainforest cousins also have magnificent foliage that makes a dramatic contrast with red and harmonises beautifully with yellow and blue. The glossy green foliage of rainforest plants such as the firewheel tree (*Stenocarpus sinuatus*) and the Illawarra flame tree (*Brachychiton acerifolius*) provide an excellent year-round backdrop for other species as well as being spectacular in their own right when flowering in spring. Clumping, strappy-leafed plants such as the mid-green spiny-headed mat rush (*Lomandra longifolia*) or the deep green stream lily (*Helmholtzia glaberimma*) make an excellent green backdrop at ground level.

Golden green foliage plants such as *Melaleuca bracteata* 'Revolution Gold' can be used to brighten the garden all year round. Other interesting variations are plants with a violet tinge to their green foliage, such as *Agonis flexuosa* 'Jervis Bay After Dark'.

White

White is light in its purest form, the sum of all the colours in the spectrum. There are many, many tones of white that have a hint of colour (often pink in flowers). White is a serene colour that blends well with just about anything. Its lack of flamboyance means that white flowers often have an additional lure for pollinators—perfume—and this is also a great attraction for gardeners. As for all colours, the effect of white is greatly influenced by what you place around it. The darker the surrounding colour, the more luminous the white flower will appear to be.

The white garden is perhaps the safest option of all. If you are confused about the many colour choices available to you, then it is hard to go wrong with an all-white garden. For the upper layer, there are a number of white-flowered eucalypts that can provide spectacular floral displays, such

Annuals such as the Swan River daisy (front) and yellow everlasting daisy can be used to create a bold statement in the garden

The blue of *Dampiera diversifolia* is complemented by a vivid blue fountain

as the red and yellow bloodwoods (*Eucalyptus* syn. *Corymbia gummifera* and *E. eximia*) or snow-in-summer (*Melaleuca linariifolia*). There are many spectacular Australian shrubs that feature white flowers, such as the baeckeas (for example, *Baeckea linifolia* and *B. virgata*), *Callistemon* 'White Anzac', the ever-blooming white form of *Grevillea banksii*, or the outstanding tea tree *Leptospermum polygalifolium* 'Cardwell'. Colour at ground level can be provided by the flowers of the native violet (*Viola hederacea*), the stream lily (*Helmholtzia glaberimma*) and the white form of *Brachyscome multifida*.

Other beautiful white-flowered plants include the creamy white *Grevillea* 'Moonlight', the white form of Geraldton wax (*Chamelaucium uncinatum*) and the wonderful climber *Pandorea jasminoides* 'Lady Di'.

Texture

Texture plays a very interesting role in the way colour is perceived. The Australian flora is rich in plants with unusual textures. For instance, there is a whole suite of species that are covered in hair. This is an adaptation to uncertain and minimal moisture levels. The dense hairs slow down the passage of water molecules from the leaves and flowers, thereby slowing evaporation. Regardless of the evolutionary significance of such features, there is an interesting effect on colour. The hairs on flowers such as kangaroo paw and flannel flower soften the colours and this in itself creates a novel look in the garden. Many of the eucalypts have silver-coloured wax coating the foliage and flower buds. This wax creates an interesting texture and once again softens the colours, in this case to silvers and silvery blues. The almost iridescent effect created is highly sought after by florists and could be used a lot more in Australian gardens by the planting

of species such as *Eucalyptus cinerea* (Argyle apple) and *E. pulverulenta* (silver-leaved mountain gum).

Many native species have relatively small flowers but plenty of them to create spectacular textural effects. An example of this is a shrub known commonly as snow-in-summer (*Myoporum floribundum*), which has masses of tiny star-like flowers sprinkled along the branches among deep green, linear leaves that hang down from the branches. This creates an interesting 'winter wonderland' kind of effect.

The woolly texture of plants such as flannel flower (*Actinotus helianthi*) not only applies to the flowers but also the foliage as it creates a wonderful, soft, silvery grey-blue appearance and texture.

Restfulness, liveliness and optical illusions

Light determines how we perceive the colour of any given object and this perception can be altered through the day as the sun moves. It can change from day to day, depending on whether we have cloudy or sunny weather. The brightest yellows and reds will be more subdued on a cloudy day, while pale-coloured flowers seem to almost glow at these times as well as at dusk.

It is worth considering at what time of day you will be regularly using your garden so you can choose colours that will work best for you. For instance, perhaps you love to come home from work and unwind in the garden; in this case, choose whites and pale pinks which tend to glow in the dark.

This last point can be particularly important in shady areas of the garden where plants such as native violet (*Viola hederacea*) and stream lily (*Helmholtzia glaberimma*) can be mass planted to make the most of the way their light-coloured flowers shine in the dull light.

Massing for colour effects

If you are looking for a simple and effective way to design with colour, then consider massed plantings of the same colour. In other words, don't just plant one of something, plant five or 10 or even more. And match it with massed plantings of other species that will create the kind of colour scheme you are looking for. This is particularly effective along borders and driveways but can also be used in other areas within garden beds. An example of this is the so-called 'meadow' plantings where seed or young seedlings are mass planted to form large, generally irregular drifts of gorgeous colour.

Colour from fruits

We usually think of flowers when we think of colour in the garden, but there are many colourful and sometimes spectacular fruits in the Australian flora that provide interesting effects, usually during those times when there is little else happening in the garden; that is, autumn and winter. Fruits often last quite a long time as well, unless of course they are discovered by birds, although this event will often also bring spectacular colours into the garden via rainbow lorikeets, rosellas and their like.

Orange tones are provided by the fruits of *Pittosporum rhombifolium*, and soothing blues by the fruits of blueberry ash (*Elaeocarpus reticulatus*), native ginger (*Alpinia caerulea*) and native flax (*Dianella caerulea*). We can also call on the dramatic purple fruits of *Callicarpa pedunculata*; the golden green, boat-like pods of the black bean tree (*Castanospermum australe*); or the greyish green immature pods of the various *Acacia* species.

Colourful foliage

Obviously, green is the main theme of foliage, but there are myriad variations on that theme and also other colours that have arisen as variegations. Interestingly hued foliage provides a way of introducing colour to the garden all year round.

Genetic changes in the growing tip of a plant can lead to variegation due to some of the tissue not producing the normal green chlorophyll pigment that is vital to the process of photosynthesis. This leads to bicoloured foliage that may be green and white or green and yellow. The overall effect of these variegated plants contrasts with the green background of normal foliage. Such effects can be particularly useful in shady situations where gardens can get a little dark and dingy. There is a versatile array of colours available among the variegated Australian plants. For example, there are the yellow–green types such as *Agonis flexuosa* 'Variegata' and *A. flexuosa* 'Belbra Gold', while the brush box (*Lophostemon confertus*) has some interesting varieties such as 'Perth Gold' and 'Variegata'.

Apart from variegations, which usually give bicoloured effects, there are also foliage variations of solid colours which can be used to create interest. *Agonis flexuosa* 'Jervis Bay After Dark', for example, has dark purple foliage that is very unusual and can be used to create wonderful colour contrasts, particularly with yellow- and white-flowered plants. The sunny yellow foliage of *Melaleuca bracteata* 'Revolution Gold' makes this a wonderful medium-sized screen plant that is beautiful in the background of an appropriate colour scheme. An interesting new addition to the range of plants with unusual coloured foliage is a dwarf blue-leafed form of kangaroo grass, *Themeda triandra* 'Mingo'.

The Australian flora has a number of plants which feature silvery grey foliage that provides a wonderfully uplifting effect in the garden. Eucalypts such as the silver-leaved mountain gum (*Eucalyptus pulverulenta*) and the Argyle apple (*E. cinerea*) can be used to provide a tall silvery background. Silver-leafed shrubs include wattles, such as

The pale mauve fragrant flowers of the white cedar (*Melia azederach*)

Lillypillies (*Acmena* and *Syzygium*) feature colourful new growth throughout the warmer months of the year

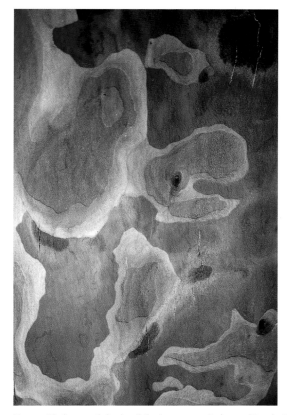

The mottled, smooth barks of the lemon-scented gum (*Eucalyptus* syn. *Corymbia citriodora*), left, and the snow gum (*Eucalyptus pauciflora*), right, can be used to create beautiful contrasts in the garden

Queensland silver wattle (*Acacia podalyriifolia*) and knifeblade acacia (*A. cultriformis*). Flannel flower (*Actinotus helianthi*) and cushion bush (*calocephalus* syn. *Lencophyta brownii*) can be used to provide a striking silver accent at ground level.

Yet another interesting foliage effect is created by the intense colours of the vigorous new growth produced by some plants during the warmer months of the year. Some examples of this include the bright purple new growth of *Acacia baileyana*, and the lillypilly group (*Acmena* and *Syzygium* species), many of which have blazing red, bronze or pink new growth. A number of new cultivars of lillypilly, such as *Syzygium* 'Blaze', have been specially selected for their spectacularly coloured growing tips.

Colour from bark

Australia is blessed with some of the most beautifully barked trees in the world. In particular, various eucalypts are prized for their bark. Most of us are familiar with the evocative images of the ghost gum from the paintings of Albert Namatjira. This species is a rather difficult one to grow away from desert climates. The alternative, if you want that sensuous smooth white bark as part of your garden, is the lemon-scented gum (*Eucalyptus* syn. *Corymbia citriodora*). For a variation on that theme, consider the spotted gum (*Eucalyptus* syn. *Corymbia maculata*), which has smooth white bark overlaid with splotches of darker-coloured bark.

Perhaps the most dramatic and gorgeous

of all is the smooth-barked apple (*Angophora costata*) with its rusty orange bark that peels away in early summer to reveal bright orange new bark. It looks absolutely stunning when the trunk is surrounded by purple-flowered plants such as the native sarsparilla (*Hardenbergia violacea*) or various native mint bushes (*Prostanthera* species). The interesting colours of this bark can be used to blend or contrast with the surrounding plants and flower colours.

The leopard tree (*Flindersia maculata*) is an excellent choice for colourful bark in more tropical or subtropical climates. Its alternating light and dark mottled bark is an unforgettable feature.

Black flowers

Black is perhaps not a colour we normally associate with flowers, but there are a number of these flowers in the Australian flora. A rather fascinating novelty, they can add drama to a colour scheme. The black kangaroo paw (*Macropidia fuliginosa*) has interesting strap-like foliage with lime green flowers that are covered in jet black hairs. The flowers can also be cut and brought indoors for an unusual arrangement.

The black coral pea (*Kennedia nigricans*) is an extremely vigorous climber so make sure you grow it in a situation where it will not choke other plants. However, its black and yellow pea-shaped flowers will add a rather different note to any colour scheme. For a dramatic contrast, try combining it with a red climber such as running postman (*Kennedia prostrata*).

The black grevillea (*Grevillea scortechinii*) is a prostrate species with flowers that are actually very dark purple but appear to be black. The spidery flowers are dotted through the foliage and these plants are perfect for containers.

Wildlife and colour attractions

The primary reason why flowers, and indeed foliage, are coloured is to attract pollinators, whether they be insects or mammals. Animals perceive colour in various ways and it is therefore not surprising that different colours attract different groups of animals. Birds, for instance, have excellent colour perception in the red range and so it is a fair bet that a red-flowered plant will be bird pollinated. This is even more likely if the plant has a tubular flower that is rich in nectar as well. A tubular flower has adapted to accommodate the long bill that most nectar-feeding birds possess.

Wildlife can be an unexpected and fleeting source of colour for the garden and there are number of choices of Australian flora for wildlife attraction. With such plants, there are many species of parrot—rosellas, lorikeets, galahs and cockatoos—that can be lured to your garden, even in heavily populated urban areas. Do not make the mistake, however, of planting brightly coloured flowers like waratahs, grevilleas and kangaroo paws at random in the garden. Try and design a colour scheme that will make sense from a design point of view in addition to catering for your feathered friends.

Hedging and topiary

There are many beautiful plants mentioned in the 'Colourful foliage' section that make superb hedges and this is a wonderful way to showcase their leaves. In particular, the various lillypillies (*Acmena* and *Syzygium* species) have really made their mark, with many compact hedging types becoming available in recent times. Other plants are also worth considering in this role: *Grevillea* 'Poorinda Peter', with its bronze-purple new growth, is an outstanding choice, as is *Leptospermum* 'Copper Sheen', which has a name that says it all.

Plants that are ever blooming

There is a select group of plants that can be used to create year-round colour in the Australian native garden. These invaluable plants can provide an excellent backbone for your colourful garden design. They can be placed in strategic positions where they will provide maximum effect for visitors to your wonderful garden.

A group of grevilleas originating from the subtropical climate of Queensland has provided a range of ever-blooming shrubs in a number of colours. White flowers are provided by the white form of *Grevillea banksii*, cream by *G.* 'Moonlight', red by *G.* 'Robyn Gordon' and *G.* 'Coconut Ice', and orange by *G.* 'Superb'. All of these shrubs are very manageable and are between 1m and 3m in height. Some of the fan flowers, including *Scaevola* 'Mauve Clusters' and *S.* 'Super Clusters', will flower virtually all year round in warmer climates. The outstanding kangaroo paws *Anigozanthos* 'Bush Ranger' and *A.* 'Bush Pearl' will also flower all year round in frost-free situations. The trick here is to remove the spent flowers and their associated fan of leaves at the base to make way for the next flush of flowers. *Thryptomene saxicola* 'Payne's Hybrid' provides dense displays of tiny pink flowers in spring and autumn but will generally have some spot flowering at other times of the year as well.

Container colour

Pots and containers of all descriptions have become increasingly popular as the size of gardens continues to shrink in urban areas. Container culture also greatly extends the range of Australian plants that can be grown in the average garden. This is due to the very good drainage that is a feature of high quality potting mixes.

Container culture also provides wonderful opportunities for the colour conscious because the containers can become decorative items in their own right, with the possibility of dressing them up in all sorts of imaginative ways. If a large number of containers is going to be used, then some sort of co-ordination of colours and textures will give a much more pleasing effect. The nursery industry has also taken the opportunity to co-ordinate flower colour with that of the container so that plants such as everlasting daisies, for instance, are now sold in matching yellow pots.

Choosing the right plant for each container situation

In order to achieve the best results, it is worth putting a little thought into matching plants and containers to your purpose. For instance, the best types of plants to consider for long-term pot culture are those that are perennial in nature but do not have large root systems, such as kangaroo paws, native violets, fan flowers (*Scaevola* species) and various native daisies, such as brachyscomes and everlasting daisies. These types of plants will continue to expand in a pot over a period of months or even years, and they have the added advantage that you can split up the plants and repot them when they have completely filled the pot. And quite shallow pots can be used for these sorts of plants, given that they do not have extensive root systems.

The smaller kangaroo paws (*Anigozanthos* species) are perfect candidates for container culture. In particular there are a number of excellent hybrids, such as 'Bush Pearl' (pink), 'Bush Ranger' (red) and 'Bush Gold' (yellow), that flower all year round in frost-free climates and these will live on indefinitely if grown in a large container. Each time the plant produces a new leaf fan, it goes straight through to flower. Just make sure you remove the old flowering stems and their associated leaves just above the potting mix surface to encourage new growth from the dormant buds at ground

Lillypillies, such as *Syzygium leuhmanii*, can be pruned to any shape or size

level. Eventually the plant will have expanded until the pot is completely full. At this stage, take the plant out of the pot and divide it into several sections, each with at least three or four leaf fans, and remove any obviously dead leaves and old flower stems before repotting each section.

Shrubs, for example the various dwarf forms of lillypilly like *Syzygium* 'Lilliput' or the smaller banksias like *Banksia* 'Birthday Candles', are suitable containers for the medium term. However, there is an issue with the root system continuing to expand each year as the plant increases in height. A point is eventually reached where the root system runs out of space and starts to die. Of course, the plant can be put into larger and larger pots each year, but this is

obviously not going to be a permanent solution. Trees, of course, are in the same boat but the problem is even worse as they tend to grow to greater heights in quicker time. Nonetheless, if we accept that some trees and shrubs may only have a limited life before they need to be replaced, then they can still be used in container gardens. They could be used to temporarily decorate an area and then be planted out in the garden before they become root bound, or simply thrown away when they have reached the limit of their useful lives. Trees and shrubs will also require much deeper pots to accommodate their deeper root systems.

Moveable colour

There are a number of Australian plants for containers that also lend themselves to being moved around and, particularly, they can be moved indoors to provide temporary colour. Many of our rainforest species are suitable in this context as they grow naturally on the rainforest floor and are very well adapted to lower light levels. Suggestions include the stream lily (*Helmholtzia glaberimma*) with its lovely creamy pink flower sprays that last for several weeks, native ginger (*Alpinia caerulea*) with its attractive bright blue fruits

Leptospermum 'Rhiannon' looks sensational grown in a container

Large containers enable us to grow species that demand perfect drainage, such as *Lechenaultia biloba* and yellow everlasting (top) and orange *Lechenaultia formosa* and yellow *Verticordia plumosa* (above)

that persist for long periods, or the native violet (*Viola hederacea*) which will continue to flower well indefinitely even under very shady conditions.

Windowboxes

Windowboxes are particularly popular in many areas of Europe where garden space is at a premium in the densely populated cities. These container gardens allow us to complement the colour scheme of the building with a splash of natural colour and texture. Indeed, the people of Europe have adopted Australian plants such as fan flower (*Scaevola* species) and brachyscome daisies with a passion and millions of these plants are being sold for their windowboxes each year.

There are a few basic pointers to success with windowboxes. We must consider the aspect of the windowbox and how much sunlight it will receive, remembering that the position of the sun varies substantially during the course of the year. In summer, the sun is much higher in the sky resulting in lots more sunlight while the opposite occurs in winter. Therefore, consider carefully the aspect as well as the colour of your wall before you choose plants to grow in your windowbox. As a result of being attached to a wall, windowboxes are often influenced by microclimatic effects, such as being protected to some degree from frosts.

Hanging baskets

There are many superb trailing plants that can be used for hanging basket culture. This also allows for a multi-level garden, maximising the use of space in limited areas and allowing displays to be created at eye level on balconies and outside windows. Plants such as the royal blue-flowering *Dampiera diversifolia*, the fan flower *Scaevola albida*, and the ground-covering grevilleas such as 'Poorinda Royal Mantle' are all ideal for this purpose.

A point to watch with both windowboxes and hanging baskets is their tendency to dry out rather quicker than plants in garden situations. This means paying extra attention to watering, although this is hardly an onerous task given the small area involved in the average windowbox.

The practicalities of container culture

Apart from the colour considerations, there are some practical points to consider about container planting. Perhaps the most important decision to make is how long term the planting will be. Is the display to last for many years or is it just a temporary planting to be disposed of when it starts to look shabby? An option is to use a fairly long-term plant such as a shrub and underplant it with a small herbaceous plant, such as a brachyscome daisy or fan flower, which can be changed at the end of its growing season.

The choice of potting mix is another crucial consideration if the planting is to reach its full potential. Always look for the Australian Standards logo on the pack, as this is a pretty good guarantee that you will have trouble-free results. It is very important for long-term plantings that you use a mix which is specifically designed for this purpose. These mixes go under various trade names such as 'Terracotta and Tub Mix'. You must also ensure that you maintain a regular feeding program with either slow-release or liquid fertilisers at recommended rates, as most potting mixes will run out of nutrients quite quickly. It is also well worth adding moisture-saving crystals or a similar product to the mix to further reduce the incidence of water stress on the plants.

The colour calendar in the native garden

One of the pleasures of gardening is watching the changes that occur through the seasons. With appropriate planning, we can create colourful displays of native plants for every season.

Summary

Summer

Christmas brings the beginning of the summer season and with it wonderful family occasions, so where better to spend this time than in the garden among some of the traditional festive Australian flowers such as New South Wales Christmas bush (*Ceratopetalum gummiferum*), Victorian Christmas bush (*Prostanthera lasianthos*) and Christmas bells (*Blandfordia* species). Western Australia has its own Christmas bush (*Nuytsia floribunda*), but it is a parasitic plant that is unfortunately extremely difficult to cultivate.

There are also many other Australian plants that can be used to create a red and green Christmas theme in the garden. For example, several of the kangaroo paws are perfect for the occasion. The red-and-green kangaroo paw (*Anigozanthos manglesii*) can be persuaded to continue flowering into the Christmas period by pruning off the older spring flowers as they finish. Various hybrid kangaroo paw varieties, such as *Anigozanthus* 'Bush Sunset', *A.* 'Bush Ranger' and *A.* 'Big Red', will also provide festive red tones in December.

For those in the southern States, the climate is perfect for the spectacular red-flowering gum (*Eucalyptus* syn. *Corymbia ficifolia*) with its blazing red flowers. The climatic range where this spectacular tree can be grown has now been greatly extended by the production of hybrids between it and a species of *Corymbia* from northern Queensland. Look for a cultivar called 'Summer Beauty' in your local garden centre or native nursery—it seems to perform well even in the hot, humid climate of Queensland.

Another glorious red-flowering plant for this time of year is the firewheel tree (*Stenocarpus sinuatus*) from Queensland, with its glossy, dark green foliage contrasting magnificently with bright red, wheel-like flowers that are well displayed.

Rosellas, rainbow lorikeets and other parrots find this species irresistible and it seems to be adaptable to most Australian climates as it will grow successfully as far south as Melbourne if given a sheltered, sunny position.

Consider also the little groundcovering plants that are not only low maintenance, and help to control weeds, but also add some subtle colour at ground level. Swamp mazus (*Mazus pumilo*) is a wonderful example of such a plant, with its masses of purplish flowers that are produced right through the summer. Another beauty is *Pratia pedunculata* with its light blue, star-like flowers adding an interesting touch of colour at ground level.

The middle of summer is a challenging time for herbaceous flowering plants in the garden. Fortunately, Australian plants are able to cope with a great deal of heat stress; however, such conditions will not usually be conducive to a wonderful flowering performance if the plants are simply left to fend for themselves. A little tender loving care, such as removing spent flowers (deadheading), using mulches, and giving plants such as scaevolas, brachyscomes and bracteanthas a weekly watering, will be well rewarded with flowering right through the summer and autumn months.

Other things that can be done in the garden during summer to encourage better flowering include:

* Prune back and fertilise New South Wales Christmas bush as the flowers drop. This will establish an excellent framework for next year's flowering.
* As kangaroo paw flowers finish, remove the flowering stem and its associated leaf fan just above ground level as this will encourage the side buds from that leaf fan to grow out and form next season's flowering display.
* Trim off spent bottlebrush flowers to just behind the old flower. Then give the plant

The pine-leaved geebung *Persoonia pinifolia* lights up the garden in autumn

* Strawflowers (*Bracteantha bracteata*)—there are numerous forms of this species, however, the annuals are very easily grown from seed and will give beautiful displays of yellow right through the warmer months. See 'Plants A to Z', pages 47–51, for more detail.
* Winged everlasting (*Ammobium alatum*)—the tall, branched flower stems add a subtlety to the spring and summer garden that is worth waiting for.
* Swan River daisy (*Brachyscome iberidifolia*)—This annual will give you a 30cm-high carpet of white, blue, mauve or purple flowers, some with black centres.

Moving on to flowering trees and shrubs, autumn marks the beginning of banksia season with some of the early-flowering species such as heath-leafed banksia (*Banksia ericifolia*) starting to flower. Ensure that your banksias are well mulched now to

a handful of slow-release native plant food to encourage a new burst of growth that will give you flowers in autumn.

Autumn

Flowering plants to consider for bringing autumn colour to your garden include croweas, banksias and pincushion hakea (*Hakea laurina*).

Autumn is also the time to start preparing your garden for the annuals that will brighten things up in spring. Native annuals such as everlasting daisies will benefit greatly from the addition of compost to the soil before planting. A few suggestions for your colourful wildflower meadow include:
* The various species of *Rhodanthe* (formerly *Helipterum*) such as *R. manglesii* and *R. chlorocephala* subsp. *rosea* (both with pink and white flowers).

Strawflowers can provide colour over many months of the year

keep moisture levels nice and even and so ensure that flowering continues well into winter. The same advice applies to the various bottlebrushes (*Callistemon* species and cultivars) and paperbarks (*Melaleuca* species and cultivars).

The many wonderful perennial herbaceous plants, such as scaevolas, brachyscomes and bracteanthas, will continue flowering right through the autumn if you continue with the tender loving care mentioned in the summer section (see page 19).

This is also the time to divide your kangaroo paws and certain other clumping plants such as flax lily (*Dianella* species). Autumn marks the beginning of the growing season for these plants and dividing them at this time will ensure a good display of flowers in the following spring and summer. Make sure that each divided section has at least three or four shoots, and it is a good idea to cut off the top one-third of the foliage to reduce water stress on the new clump while it re-establishes itself.

Winter

Winter is a season of more subdued light, yet there is still an abundance of flowers to brighten the garden at this time. And in fact many native plants are at their best.

Mid-winter in most parts of Australia is generally a quiet time in the garden, however with a little imagination we can still create colourful displays. One of the highlights in the garden at this time is undoubtedly the winter-flowering wattles, particularly the Cootamundra wattle (*Acacia baileyana*) and the Queensland silver wattle (*A. podalyriifolia*), with both species providing a bold dash of golden yellow.

Banksias reach their absolute prime during winter and some excellent choices include the coast banksia (*Banksia integrifolia*) with its lemon yellow flowers, hairpin banksia (*B. spinulosa*) with its yellow-orange flowers, and *Banksia* 'Giant Candles' which is a spectacular large-flowered hybrid that is irresistible to birds. There are also a number of interesting dwarf cultivars for the smaller garden or

Cutleaf daisy (*Brachyscome multifida*) and flannel flower (*Actinotus helianthi*) are perfect from spring to summer

courtyard, such as 'Birthday Candles', 'Australflora Pygmy Possum', 'Stumpy Gold', 'Mini Marg' and 'Honey Pots'. These dwarf types have been selected from a wide range of species therefore it is best to consult the 'Plants A to Z' section, where full details are given so that you can select the best ones for your garden.

Correa is another group of plants that reaches its flowering peak in wintertime. The lovely pendent tubular flowers are dotted through pleasant foliage and some of the best choices include *Correa reflexa* in all its many forms; *C. alba*, a beautiful white-flowered species that is great for coastal areas; and *C. pulchella* with its pinkish bell-shaped flowers.

Winter is also the time when many colourful native plants are getting ready for their big spring displays and it is vital to look after them by keeping them well watered if you want them to reach their full potential. For most of the spring-flowering shrubs, it is a case of 'steady as she goes' as too much tender loving care can backfire. In particular, it is important not to fertilise shrubs such as Geraldton wax, boronia and New South Wales Christmas bush as this can stimulate vegetative growth that will hide the flowers. Generally speaking, the best thing you can do in winter is keep your plants well mulched and ensure that the soil does not dry out.

Spring

Virtually anything goes in spring as the choice of colourful flowering plants is seemingly endless. Perhaps the secret here is to decide to limit yourself in spring so that there is plenty of space in your garden for plants that flower at other times of the year. Spring-flowering shrubs form the backbone of most gardens and the trick is to choose ones that will be long lived in your climate. For instance, Geraldton wax (*Chamelaucium* species) and Swan River myrtle

(*Hypocalymma robustum*) are the perfect choices for the hot dry summers of Perth or Adelaide but they are generally not reliable in Sydney. A better choice for the warmer, more humid climates of the central and northern eastern coastal regions are plants such as bottlebrush (*Callistemon* species and cultivars), baeckea and tea tree (*Leptospermum* species and cultivars).

Waratahs (*Telopea* species and cultivars) are the ideal plants to make a bold spring statement in southeastern Australia. Other red-flowering plants to consider are the crimson kunzea (*Kunzea baxteri*) and running postman (*Kennedia prostrata*). For white flowers consider flannel flower (*Actinotus* species), willow-myrtle (*Agonis* species) and *Callistemon* 'White Anzac'. Bold purple flowers can be supplied by happy wanderer (*Hardenbergia violacea*) and native mint bushes (*Prostanthera* species). Pink flowers can come from the wax flower *Eriostemon australasius* or pink forms of Geraldton wax, while orange flowers can come from flame peas (*Chorizema* species). Finally, for yellows there are cottonheads (*Conostylis* species) and various species of *Phebalium*.

The most important maintenance task for a colourful garden in spring is pruning. First, make sure you remove spent flowers as soon as practical as this can sometimes encourage a second burst of flowering later in spring. Second, when all flowering is finished, give your spring-flowering shrubs a trim, cutting back to just below where the flowers have been. This will make the plant even more bushy and floriferous in the following year.

Pruning to encourage year-round colour

Pruning of your plants is the key to ensuring maximum colour in your garden all year round. The method used for pruning will depend on two main factors:

❋ The age of the plant. Ideally, if you want a compact plant covered with flowers, you should start pruning from the beginning of the growing season. Pinch out the growing tips of the plant several times throughout the growing season as discussed in the following section on tip-pruning. On the other hand, if a plant has been let go for a few years and has become too leggy, then see the section on renovation pruning opposite.

❋ The stage of the flowering season for the particular species. Deadheading of old flowers should be done during the flowering period and should be followed by a general tidy at the end of flowering (see the following sections).

We'll start with the simpler pruning techniques and work through to the more advanced ideas.

Deadheading
This technique is particularly useful for long-flowering herbaceous plants such as scaevolas (fan flowers), brachyscome daisies and strawflowers (*Bracteantha* species). Flowering often goes on for many months and deadheading simply means pinching out with finger and thumb the old flowers as they wither and die. This process not only greatly improves the appearance of the plant but also directs the energies of the plant into producing more flowers rather than fruits and seeds.

Tip-pruning
One of the secrets of having a lot more flowers on your plants lies in first creating an extensive vegetative framework. Any plant will benefit from tip-pruning but it is particularly effective with woody plants. For both herbaceous and woody plants, the removal of the growing tip by pinching it out between finger and thumb encourages the dormant buds immediately below it to grow out, thus producing many shoots where previously there was only one. This in turn leads to many more flowers when those shoots eventually reach the flowering stage. The trick with tip-pruning is to do it throughout the growing season.

After-flowering pruning
A good general rule with flowering shrubs and trees is to prune them straight after flowering. The reason for this is that many woody plants start a spurt of growth immediately after flowering has finished. If left unpruned, they will simply continue to add growth onto the flowering stems and this leads to the plants becoming excessively leggy. The amount of wood to remove when pruning is very much dependent on the plant type.

Renovation pruning
Most Australian plants are very forgiving and can be pruned back as hard as you like without killing the plant. This is because most woody native plants are adapted to regeneration from bushfires, which often raze them to ground level. They then grow back from an underground stem called a lignotuber. The resulting growth from this structure is very vigorous and soft, and it will generally not flower in the first year after such hard pruning. Renovation pruning will, however, create a vigorous bushy plant that will remain compact if pruned lightly after it starts flowering again.

Renovation pruning is particularly effective for plants that have a lignotuber, such as banksias, waratahs, tea trees and most other woody Australian plants. The only major exception is plants in the pea family, such as wattles.

Plants A to Z

Acacia species and cultivars (wattles)

It is one of the classic bits of folklore on Australian plants that it does not matter what month of the year it is, there will always be a wattle of some sort in flower. However, caution needs to be exercised with all the wattles because they are very adaptable, hardy plants that can often seed themselves in surrounding bushland and displace the indigenous flora there.

Acacia baileyana (Cootamundra wattle)
With its silvery grey, feathery foliage, the Cootamundra wattle is arguably the most popular but perhaps also the most controversial wattle in cultivation as it commonly escapes from gardens. Nonetheless, in urban areas where it cannot invade the bush, it is still a useful plant. It

Acacia baileyana 'Purpurea'

Above: The bright yellow flowers of the Queensland silver wattle (*Acacia podalyriifolia*) will light up those dull winter days

Opposite: Red and green kangaroo paw (*Anigozanthos manglesii*)

flowers profusely around July and August and can provide a wonderful backdrop for smaller plants. The species grows to a height of up to 8m and can spread to a similar diameter. It is also drought and frost resistant. *Acacia baileyana* 'Purpurea' is a wonderful purple-leafed variant of this species. Its new growth shows the most intense colour, and this can provide year-round contrast between the older grey-green foliage and the purple tips. There is also a groundcovering form, sometimes sold as *A. baileyana* 'Prostrate Form', which is great value in rockeries and large containers.

Acacia cultriformis (knifeblade acacia)
The interesting shape of the soft, greyish green foliage gives this plant its common name. Golden ball-shaped flowers are borne in profusion in spring. It grows to about 3m tall and wide, and the foliage colour makes it an ideal background plant in the garden. It is also very drought and frost tolerant.

Acacia podalyriifolia (Queensland silver wattle)
This is one of the most ornamental of all the wattles, with its silvery green foliage and bright yellow winter flowers. It is also relatively compact, growing to about 5m tall by 2–3m wide. Its only major problem is its tendency to seed readily and escape from cultivation, however seedlings are easily removed. It is also drought and frost tolerant.

Acmena smithii (lillypilly)
One way to provide some unusual colour is by planting any of the various lillypillies (*Acmena* and *Syzygium*) that offer seasonal whites, pinks and reds with their edible fruits and glossy dark green foliage year-round. Without doubt, one of the best and most versatile of the group is *Acmena smithii*, which comes in a number of shapes and sizes from a low-growing shrub to a

spreading tree that grows to 20m in height. The usual form of *A. smithii* is a small to medium-sized tree; however, for smaller gardens the creek lillypilly (a narrow-leafed or rheophytic form of *A. smithii*) is a very rewarding plant because it is a compact shrub, 3–4m in height, that has reddish new growth and also produces pink- to mauve-coloured fruits that are held right through into winter. It is extremely adaptable to different soils and climatic conditions, and will stand light frost. Best of all, though, is its capacity to respond to hard pruning, which means it works well as a hedge or topiary specimen. Indeed, a dwarf selection called 'Hedgemaster' grows to only 1m in height. Good forms of the creek lillypilly can be readily struck from firm tip-cuttings.

Actinotus species (flannel flowers)
The beautiful creamy white flowers of these classic Australian plants add a rather unique texture to the garden.

Actinotus helianthi (flannel flower)
The silvery white flowers and grey-green foliage of this species make it an excellent plant for those wishing to create a garden in these subdued colours. It is often, however, a difficult plant to establish in the garden as it prefers very well-drained, sandy soils such as those found in the coastal heathlands that are its natural habitat. Full sun or very light shade will give the best results and the plant can withstand mild frost. New varieties or cultivars of flannel flower such as 'Federation Star' (recently released by the Royal Botanic Gardens in Sydney) are becoming widely available and are worth trying in the garden. However, it is best to consider the flannel flower as a plant that should be replaced after a year or so. Although some forms of the flannel flower will grow for several years and form a small shrub, mostly they are short-lived and will only grow to perhaps 50cm high and wide.

Adenanthos sericea (woollybush)

This shrub has wonderful silvery green, silky foliage that creates a striking effect in any garden. In fact, most people find the tactile experience of stroking the foliage to be irresistible. This plant is best suited to growing in the more Mediterranean climates of the southern States of Australia. It prefers full sun and good drainage, and should be lightly pruned after flowering. Under ideal conditions, it will grow to 4–5m tall and wide. It is relatively frost tolerant and is quick growing, making it a good choice as a screening or hedge plant.

Agonis species (willow-myrtles)

These adaptable members of the eucalyptus family provide lovely displays of masses of tiny white flowers in spring.

Agonis flexuosa (willow-myrtle, peppermint tree)

This plant is a 'tough-as-nails', medium-sized tree from the near-coastal areas of southwestern Western Australia. The lime green foliage makes a nice backdrop for the sprays of white flowers that look like a sprinkling of snow when they appear in spring. The leaves have a spicy peppermint perfume when crushed and the tree is frost hardy. For the lover of variegated plants, there is also a cultivar (*Agonis flexuosa* 'Variegata') which is rather slow growing and is smaller than the normal green form.

Agonis parviceps

This is a small to medium-sized shrub that adapts well to conditions of poor drainage and still produces its massed display of small, white, starry flowers right throughout late winter and spring. With its dense foliage, it is a lovely option for a screen plant.

Alpinia species (native gingers)

Gardeners in the warmer areas of Australia have many interesting native rainforest plants that are ideal for their situations. The native gingers have soothing, dark green foliage and rather subtle flowers and fruits that will add an unusual touch to your colour scheme. All the gingers come from tropical or subtropical climates and will not tolerate frost at all. They will thrive in a shady position in the garden that has a cool root run, something that can be provided by growing them under trees or by providing extensive mulching around them. The various native gingers are all easily increased by dividing the clumps in autumn.

Alpinia arctiflora (booroogun)

This is a rather robust species that will grow to 3–4m tall and form a clump several metres wide. It has delicate white flowers that are pink in bud in autumn and unusually coloured mauve-brown fruits throughout autumn and winter. It may take a little time and effort to track down this plant in the nursery trade.

Alpinia caerulea (native ginger)

This much smaller ginger, growing to about 1–2m high and wide, has white flowers and gorgeous blue fruits that may be borne at any time of the year. Its smaller stature makes it an interesting pot specimen. Some nurseries carry an interesting form of this species that has maroon-red undersides to the leaf.

Ammobium alatum (winged everlasting)

This plant is sometimes known as poached-egg everlasting because of its fascinating, pure white, bracted flowers that have an orange-yellow centre. Seed is planted in the autumn and this is rewarded by massed displays of flowers from spring into autumn. It forms a clump of dense, rosetted foliage and sends up branched flower stems that bear numerous small daisy flowers. It is best grown as an annual and is quite frost tolerant.

Creek lillypilly (*Acmena smithii*)

Flannel flower (*Actinotus helianthi*)

Various colour forms of the evergreen kangaroo paw (*Anigozantos flavidus*), a virtually indestructible performer

Angophora species

The angophoras add a subtle wave of colour to the garden with their large, profuse, cream-coloured flowers in summer. They are generally rather underrated as garden plants and the dwarf apple gum (*Angophora hispida*) in particular deserves to be planted more widely.

Angophora costata (smooth-barked apple)
This majestic tree, also known as the Sydney red gum, is without doubt one of the world's most beautiful trees with its wonderfully gnarled trunk being clothed in rusty orange, smooth bark that is shed each summer. It can grow up to 25m tall by 15m wide, although there is a dwarf cultivar (detailed below). The fresh bark is a very intense colour, and this gradually fades throughout the year until the bark is renewed. Around the same time as the bark is shed, the canopy is covered in cream-coloured, honey-scented blossoms. This species is rather susceptible to frosts but will withstand coastal conditions reasonably well. It does not need to be pruned, in fact it is best to simply allow it to form its own shape. The exciting new dwarf cultivar known as *Angophora costata* 'Little Gum Ball' reputedly grows to only a few metres tall and is covered throughout the warmer months in bright red new foliage growth.

Angophora hispida (dwarf apple gum)
This plant can grow as a shrub or small tree and may be 3–10m in height and 3–6m wide. It naturally inhabits poorly drained rock shelves in the sandstone country centred on the Sydney region and will therefore adapt quite well to a range of drainage conditions. This species is rather susceptible to frosts and requires maximum sunlight to flower well. Unlike its taller cousin, the smooth-barked apple, it should be pruned quite heavily after flowering if you would like it to form a compact and spectacular flowering shrub. The flowers, buds and foliage are used by commercial florists, and this is also an added attraction for the home gardener.

Anigozanthos species and cultivars (kangaroo paws)

The iridescent colours of this spectacular group are hard to go past if you want to create bold strokes of colour in your garden. There are two basic rules to obey to ensure success with the cultivation of kangaroo paws—full sun and good drainage. After flowering, it is essential to remove the old flower stems as low to the ground as possible; this makes way for the next flush of leaf growth that will eventually produce the next crop of flowers. It is also vital to

The exquisite form and bark of *Angophora costata*

give the plants an even supply of water during the active growth period from autumn until flowering occurs, and they especially need plenty of water during late winter and spring when the flower buds are rapidly expanding. A handful of slow-release fertiliser spread around the base of the plant in mid-autumn will also greatly assist the formation of flowers.

Anigozanthos flavidus
(evergreen kangaroo paw)
This must be one of the toughest ornamental plants to grace the surface of the earth. It is well worth thinking about a collection of the various forms of this species. It has numerous colour forms including red, pink, orange, light green, yellow, red and green, maroon, and even very rare, creamy white types. It also varies markedly in height between different forms from the compact 1m or so tall to the gigantic (up to 4m!). It has bright green, strap-like leaves that are extremely tough and resistant to most pests and diseases. The various hybrid kangaroo paws have tended to lessen the demand for this species, however it is well worth seeking the better forms of this species at specialist native nurseries.

Anigozanthos manglesii (red-and-green kangaroo paw)
It is hard to imagine a more vibrant colour combination than the red and green of this most famous of all the kangaroo paws. It can be readily grown in the home garden, particularly in pots, but should be considered an annual or short-lived perennial. If seed is raised in spring or summer, a brilliant flowering display will be achieved the following spring. The plant is not, however, particularly frost hardy and is rather susceptible to snail damage and a problem known as ink spot. The best remedy for ink spot is removal of blackened leaves as they appear.

Anigozanthos cultivars
Advances in the breeding of kangaroo paws have led to an explosion in the number of new cultivars available to gardeners. There is now tremendous variation in size, shape and colour as well as a general improvement in hardiness, although it must be said that they are still as a group not yet perfect in this regard. The best improvement of all, however, has been the development of cultivars with extremely long flowering periods—including a number of cultivars that are ever blooming in frost-free climates.

The tall and medium-sized kangaroo paw cultivars listed below are all very adaptable plants and suitable for the temperate regions of Australia. They will thrive in most soil types provided the soil is not completely waterlogged.

We can divide the kangaroo paws into several different groups according to height and flowering period.

Tall cultivars (2m and more)
These cultivars are all based on a very hardy species called *Anigozanthos flavidus*. This species has very tough, strappy, bright green leaves that have a somewhat leathery texture and this characteristic has been passed on to its hybrids in a very uniform way. This seems to make them virtually indestructible in most garden situations. This group features flower stems that are 1.5–2m tall, and has flowers in a wide range of colours.

Anigozanthos 'Bush Dawn'
This cultivar has strappy mid-green leaves about 1.2m long, with 2m-tall profusely branched flower stems bearing masses of small, bright yellow flowers. The flowers are produced in late spring to early summer. The clump will potentially reach 1m or more in width under good growing conditions. This plant is a wonderful addition to any garden as it is one of the toughest and most consistent performers of all the hybrid

kangaroo paws. It can easily produce 50 to 100 stems of its vibrant yellow flowers—a spectacular display indeed.

Anigozanthos 'Bush Sunset'
Slightly more compact and flowering earlier than 'Bush Dawn', this cultivar has strappy, mid-green leaves about 1m long and profusely branched flower stems 1.5–1.8m tall. The clump will potentially reach 1m or more in width under good growing conditions and the plant lives for many years. This cultivar is a wonderful, bright red kangaroo paw that is the obvious companion to 'Bush Dawn'; and they do make a wonderful contrast to each other when planted in the same area of a garden. It shares the hardiness of 'Bush Dawn' as well.

Anigozanthos flavidus 'Flashpoint'
This fascinating cultivar has 1m-long leaves that have an unusual yellow-striped variegation. The bright orange flowers are borne on 1.8–2m stems and also have variegation, making them a spectacular complement to the foliage. This is a very tough and long-lived plant that will tolerate frost to a slight degree.

Medium-sized cultivars
These grow to about 1m in height and flower from spring through early summer.

Anigozanthos 'Bush Gold'
This cultivar has short (60cm), stiff, upright mid-green leaves with 1m-tall, sparsely branched flower stems bearing masses of small, bright yellow flowers throughout spring and summer and sporadically at other times of the year. The clump will potentially reach a spread of about 50cm or more under good growing conditions. The vibrant yellow flowers of this cultivar coupled with its vigour have made it popular commercially. It is highly recommended as one of the toughest of all the hybrid kangaroo paw cultivars.

Anigozanthos 'Pink Joey'
Similar in stature to 'Bush Gold', this cultivar has short (60cm), strappy, dark green leaves with 1m-tall, profusely branched flower stems bearing lots of small, bright pink flowers in late spring and early summer. The clump will potentially reach a spread of about 1m wide under good growing conditions. This plant was for many years the only widely available kangaroo paw cultivar. It is quite hardy and the soft pink flowers blend well with many other plants. Its only major drawback is that its flowering season is much shorter than many of the other small to medium-sized cultivars available. It does, however, look tremendous as a potted specimen.

Dwarf cultivars
There are many lovely dwarf kangaroo paws that are ideal for the smaller garden.

Anigozanthos 'Bush Pearl'
This is a relatively recent, ever-blooming type that has branched flower stems to about 1m in height and lovely soft pink flowers. The plant itself will spread to about 30cm wide with mid-green foliage that has proved to be rather tough.

Anigozanthos 'Bush Ranger'
This is a dwarf type (50cm tall) with strappy, mid-green leaves and profusely branched flower stems, 60–70cm tall, bearing masses of small, bright red flowers throughout the year provided no frosts are experienced. The clump will potentially reach a spread of about 40cm wide under good growing conditions. This is a plant suitable for the temperate regions of Australia but it requires good drainage and full sun in order to thrive. It needs plenty of water during the warmer months of the year when the flower buds are rapidly expanding. This hybrid represented a real breeding breakthrough in kangaroo paws

Anigozanthus 'Bush Dawn'

Anigozanthus 'Bush Ranger'

Lemon-scented myrtle (*Backhousia citriodora*)

with its ever-blooming habit. In frost-free climates, it just goes on and on producing its flame red flowers.

Astartea 'Winter Pink'

This is an extremely lovely, small shrub that will add a dash of pink to the winter garden. It comes from the myrtle family (Myrtaceae) and is a compact plant, growing to about 1m in height and width, and has masses of pink star-shaped flowers in winter. It does like good drainage and full sun and ideally you should prune it by cutting long stems for use in the vase. This will further assist in keeping the plants nice and bushy.

Backhousia species

This genus from the myrtle family (Myrtaceae) includes several species that will add beautiful creamy white flowers and fantastic glossy, dark green foliage to the garden. The aniseed myrtle (*Backhousia anisata*) and the lemon-scented myrtle (*B. citriodora*) are two very aromatic plants that grow in the rainforests of northeastern Australia. The beautiful, densely packed, glossy green foliage makes both these species worth planting for their leaves alone.

You will be thinking about licorice when you crush the leaf of the aniseed myrtle. Under ideal conditions, this plant can reach 10m in height and forms a bushy, small tree that is 4–5m wide. The shiny leaves have an attractive wavy margin, and the clusters of mildly fragrant flowers are an additional feature in mid- to late spring. The leaves of the aniseed myrtle can also be dried and crushed and used to brew a truly unique cup of tea.

The lemon-scented myrtle grows to a similar height and diameter as the aniseed

Aniseed myrtle (*Backhousia anisata*)

tree, and as an added bonus it has one of the strongest lemon leaf fragrances of any plant you are likely to encounter anywhere. It usually forms a compact large shrub or small tree, and has noticeable clusters of small, white flowers in early summer.

Both these backhousias make excellent screen species and, being rainforest species, they can also cope quite well with shade from taller trees. However, don't expect them to be frost tolerant.

Baeckea species

These rather subtle members of the myrtle family (Myrtaceae) usually have masses of tiny white or pink flowers. They are generally hardy, reliable plants that blend beautifully into the native garden. All baeckeas benefit from a light prune after flowering. Most species are not very tolerant of frost.

Baeckea camphorata
This adaptable, compact shrub grows to 2–3m high and presents a showy display of white in mid-spring. Its interesting foliage is pleasantly perfumed with the odour of camphor, as its name suggests.

Baeckea linifolia
The dark green needle-like foliage of this 1.5–2m shrub is interesting for its effect alone. It adapts particularly well to moist soils and will tolerate less than perfect drainage. In spring, there is a subtle but significant display of tiny white flowers.

Baeckea syn. Babbingtonia virgata
This is normally a substantial shrub that grows up to 4m or more in height by a similar spread. There are, however, some fantastic dwarf forms of this species that are available as cultivars. 'Howie's Sweet Midget' grows into a dense, bun-shaped plant no more than 1m or so high by a similar width. It is sprinkled with tiny white flowers in spring, and is an ideal plant for courtyards

and containers with its dense, feathery foliage providing a soothing backdrop in the garden. It is also excellent for small hedges and topiary work.

Banksia species and cultivars

Winter is one of those quiet times in the garden when there is a general lack of colour. The banksias are the perfect group of plants to fill that gap as their main flowering period encompasses those difficult cooler months. They are certainly one of the first plants to think about as the backbone for your bush garden in winter. There are about 70 species of banksia with all but one being exclusively indigenous to Australia; *Banksia dentata* actually extends into the tropical climate of New Guinea. While there are a number of spring- to summer-flowering banksias, particularly in Western Australia, there is a significant number of winter-flowering species as well, with many from the eastern States. For those who cannot accommodate the larger banksias described below, there are a number of low-growing cultivars that only grow to about 1m or less in height and are ideal for rockeries or, even better, large pots.

The banksias are an extremely diverse group of species that are found from mountain peaks right down to the windswept cliffs and dunes around the Australian coastline. Some species grow in perfectly drained sandy soils while others grow in heavy clay soils and still others, such as the swamp banksia (*Banksia robur*), are able to thrive in boggy swamps, an ability that also translates into the garden. There are also tree species such as old man banksia (*B. serrata*) and coast banksia (*B. integrifolia*), and shrubby species such as hairpin banksia (*B. spinulosa*). So there is a banksia species to suit virtually every climate and garden in Australia.

An exciting development in the last decade has been the selection of many dwarf cultivars which are much better suited to the smaller gardens that are the trend in modern urban areas. Many of these selections originate from coastal headlands where the windy conditions apparently suit the lower-growing or prostrate forms of various species, and this habit is genetically maintained when these forms are grown in garden situations.

The various banksias have such different growing requirements that you should refer to the individual growing notes below for each species and cultivar.

Banksia ericifolia (heath-leaved banksia)
The heath-leaved banksia (*Banksia ericifolia*) is a very adaptable species, probably due to the fact that it occurs naturally in fairly swampy heathlands in eastern Australia. It makes a great screen plant, growing several metres high by the same width. And not only does it provide copious nectar for honey-eating birds, its dense foliage also provides nesting possibilities for them. It normally has orange flowers but other colour variations such as maroon are becoming available in the nursery trade.

Banksia integrifolia (coast banksia)
The coast banksia forms a medium-sized tree, up to 15–20m tall, and can be found in the wild from tropical Queensland right down the east coast to the cool climate of Tasmania. Its extensive range indicates its adaptability—it can withstand the strong winds and salt spray of the coast but is also equally hardy in heavier soils and with the frosts of inland regions. Its lemon yellow flower spikes are smaller than many other banksias, but they are still very noticeable and are attractive to birdlife. Another feature from a colour point of view is the silvery underside of the leaf, which is prominently displayed when the canopy blows around in the wind, giving an interesting two-tone effect to the foliage.

Banksia robur (swamp banksia)
This spectacular banksia can reach 2m in height by a similar spread. Its great claim to fame is its ability to thrive in very poorly drained soils, making it a very useful garden plant. It has large, dark green, shiny leaves and is peppered all year with a succession of blooms. The flower bud is a very unusual blue-green colour and develops into a large, lemon yellow flower head. This species is also fairly frost tolerant.

Banksia serrata (old man banksia)
This rather gnarly tree banksia will introduce some interesting texture to your garden as well as light green foliage and silvery yellow flowers. It does grow into a medium-sized tree up to 20m high by 10m wide and requires a well-drained soil in maximum sunlight. It makes a great background plant.

Banksia spinulosa (hairpin banksia)
This fantastic shrub usually grows to a height of a couple of metres by a similar width, and is covered in spectacular flowers from February to July. It is an excellent plant for growing under established eucalypts, and responds very well to pruning after flowering. There are a few interesting dwarf cultivars of this species, two of which are listed later in this section (see page 38).

Banksia cultivars

There are many wonderful *Banksia* cultivars that have been selected for their excellent performance in cultivation.

Banksia 'Giant Candles'
This is an outstanding cultivar that forms a tall shrub 4–5m in height and will grow to a similar width if left unpruned. Thin, linear leaves are densely arranged on the branches which are also studded with the long flower spikes, often more than 40cm in length,

with the dark-coloured styles providing a strong contrast with the yellow background of the flower. The bold flower spikes are produced throughout autumn and winter and maintain their beauty for many weeks. This plant is quite adaptable to a range of soil types and can cope with less than perfect drainage, a characteristic that is presumably inherited from one of its parents, *Banksia ericifolia,* which commonly inhabits wet heathland areas. Low-phosphorus native plant fertilisers should be used in autumn and spring for maximum flower production. This cultivar seems to be particularly hungry for extra iron, as shown by the yellow tips which often develop at the ends of the branches. This can be

corrected by a dose of chelated iron at the manufacturer's recommended rates. It may be a bit touchy about heavy pruning so the best strategy is to tip-prune the plant from the beginning. 'Giant Candles' is a great bird-attracting plant, but be prepared to give it plenty of room to move or else shape it by pruning each year to keep it compact.

Dwarf banksias

The keen native gardener can now choose from a swag of low-growing banksias that are ideal for rockeries, borders, containers or as groundcovers. A selection of the best new cultivars is provided below. All the cultivars are extremely attractive to birds, with the added bonus that they are at a height where they can be more readily enjoyed by the human eye.

Banksia integrifolia 'Australflora Roller Coaster'
This is a prostrate form of the coast banksia, normally a small to medium-sized tree. 'Australflora Roller Coaster' grows to only 20cm high but spreads to a width of about 2.5m and can be made to cascade down banks or over the edge of a large pot. It has large, dark green, silver-backed leaves and produces lots of lemon yellow brushes throughout winter and sporadically at other times of the year. It is very adaptable to a wide range of conditions as *Banksia integrifolia* is one of the most widely distributed and hardiest of all the banksias. It will even thrive in exposed coastal conditions. It can also be planted inland where it will tolerate light frosts. It is a plant that requires as much sun as possible and will also attract birds. This is a very useful selection of one of the easiest to grow of all the banksias thanks to its outstanding garden performance, not to mention its attractive flower display. It may be a bit difficult to track down but it will be well worth the effort.

Baeckea camphorata

Coast banksia (*B. integrifolia*)

River dog rose (*Bauera rubioides*), a fantastic plant that flowers well in moist, shady positions

Banksia marginata 'Mini Marg'
This is a very compact, bushy shrub that grows to a height of about 30cm and spreads to more than 1m wide. It becomes covered with bright lemon yellow, bird-attracting flower spikes during the summer and autumn months. It grows best in well-drained soils, in either full sun or slightly shaded positions. It will readily tolerate drought and exposure to coastal conditions. This is not surprising as 'Mini Marg' is a dwarf selection of *Banksia marginata* which originated on the north coast of Tasmania.

Banksia serrata 'Australflora Pygmy Possum'
This is a prostrate form of what is normally a large shrub or small tree. This cultivar grows to only 30cm high but spreads to a width of 2–3m. It has stiff, serrated, mid-green leaves and its yellow flower spikes are displayed prominently above the foliage. Flowers are produced throughout spring and summer. Anyone familiar with the normal tree form of *Banksia serrata,* the classic old man banksia, will want 'Australflora Pygmy Possum'. This cultivar, like the other prostrate banksia forms, makes an ideal potted plant. It would also be very suitable for rockery plantings and will tolerate harsh coastal conditions.

Banksia spinulosa 'Birthday Candles'
This dwarf shrub grows to about 45cm high and up to 1m wide. It features fine, crowded, linear leaves, and a showy display of gold flowers with dark red styles from early autumn through to late winter. It is a very hardy plant that requires full sun and good drainage. It will tolerate light frosts and has adapted well to gardens from Brisbane through to Melbourne.

Banksia spinulosa 'Stumpy Gold'
This is a stout, low-growing shrub or semi-groundcover growing to about 40cm tall and 1.2m wide. It features golden flower spikes 30–40cm long that project through the foliage from mid-autumn until early spring. It grows best in well-drained soils in either full sun or slightly shaded positions. This form is hardy to moderate frosts once established.

Bauera rubioides (river dog rose)

The river dog rose is one of those very handy plants that will flower well in fairly shady conditions. While it can be pruned to any shape or size you require, it will reach a height of about 1.5–2m if left unpruned. It has deep green, fine foliage that provides a useful background colour, and the pink or white flowers are produced in profusion over a very long period throughout spring and summer. Its normal habitat is a permanently moist soil along a creek or river bank, so try to duplicate these conditions in your garden for best results.

Blandfordia species (Christmas bells)

The Christmas bells (various *Blandfordia* species) fit the bill perfectly with their waxy, fiery red and yellow flowers that hang down in a pendulous fashion and are reminiscent of bells. These fascinating plants are actually members of the lily family (Liliaceae) and there are four different kinds, with one in Tasmania and three others that occur from central coastal New South Wales up to the coastal areas of Queensland. They tend to grow mainly in swampy country in the wild, and have proved themselves to be adaptable to cultivation and are particularly well suited to pot culture. They are easily propagated from fresh seed that should be sown in a normal seed-raising mix.

The biggest problem with growing Christmas bells is that they have but a few wispy grass-like leaves which can easily get lost under a carpet of weeds. Therefore the best thing is to grow them in pots until they are really well established, and take care to mulch around the base of the plant even if it is in a pot. A good feed of slow-release native plant food in spring will also help to keep your plants vigorous and get them into flower as soon as possible. With regard to flowering, you will need to be patient as it can take several or more years for the plants to get big enough to flower.

One very interesting aspect of growing Christmas bells is the way they flower profusely in the season after a bush fire. This suggests a couple of things to the gardener—either that you should singe the plant a few months before you want it to flower, or perhaps try a special dose of potash fertiliser to simulate the nutrients released after a fire. You can provide potash by sprinkling a heaped teaspoon of sulphate of potash (potassium sulphate) around the base of the plant and watering in well. Perhaps the best of all the Christmas bells in cultivation is *Blandfordia grandiflora*, which has very large flowers that can vary in colour from seedling to seedling from dark red and yellow to pure yellow.

Boronia species and cultivars

Boronias belong to the family Rutaceae and so are part of the citrus group, a fact that may surprise. However, the delicious perfume of the flowers of several of the boronias is somewhat reminiscent of the beautiful scent of orange blossoms.

Boronia heterophylla (red boronia)
This is a bushy shrub that grows to 2m high and wide. It has beautiful, dark green ferny leaves and is covered in fragrant, bright reddish pink flowers throughout spring. It is reasonably adaptable and grows well under established eucalypts if given an adequate supply of moisture during the growing season. It will also withstand light to medium frosts. A beautiful compact form with pale pink flowers has been released as *Boronia heterophylla* 'Just Margaret' and is worth seeking out.

Boronia megastigma (brown boronia)
Perhaps the best of the perfumed boronias is a plant that has been popular for decades, especially in Melbourne where the suburb Boronia was named for the extensive area planted with brown boronia for the cut flower trade. Brown boronia can reach a height of up to 2m by 1m wide and is best grown in regions of Australia that have low summer rainfall as this will mimic the natural conditions that the plant experiences in the wild in southwestern Western Australia. If you want to grow it in more humid climates such as Sydney, then it may be best to try pot culture—growing the plant in a pot gives immaculate drainage. A number of interesting colour forms have been named over the years and some are still available from specialist native nurseries; for instance, 'Harlequin' has brown and yellow striped flowers, and 'Chandleri' has rich burgundy flowers.

Boronia serrulata (Sydney rock rose)
Another boronia that cannot be ignored is the Sydney rock rose, which derives its common name from the floral perfume that is reminiscent of some of the best fragrant roses. It grows to about 1m in height and width, and has an unusual serrated leaf that also has a strong perfume. It must be said that this species is not a robust plant in cultivation; however, if you are prepared to grow it in a large pot, good results can usually be achieved. It is a plant that grows among sandstone outcrops in dappled shade with very well-drained, sandy soil as a growing medium. Re-creating this in your garden or container will be the best way to grow this and other boronias.

Boronia 'Tyalge Ruby'
This is a very attractive, small shrub that grows to approximately 1m high and wide. It features ferny, lemon-scented foliage, and masses of pink flowers that fade to white

Christmas bell (*Blandfordia grandiflora*)

Boronia heterophylla requires excellent drainage but is worth the effort

The perfumes of the brown boronia (*B. megastigma*), top, and Sydney rock rose (*B. serrulata*), above, are exquisite during winter and spring. It prefers moist, well-drained soils with some overhead protection but will tolerate full sun. This plant is reputedly much hardier than the common brown boronia and will tolerate drier conditions. It is an excellent plant under windows or in borders where the aromatic lemon foliage and long flowering habit can be best appreciated. 'Tyalge Ruby' also makes an ideal container plant as well as being an attractive cut flower for small posies. Its use as a cut flower will serve to prune the plant and keep it nice and bushy. This rather intriguing new cultivar is a hybrid between *Boronia citriodora* and *B. muelleri* and it originated in Alvina Smith's native garden at Tynong, Victoria.

Brachychiton acerifolius (Illawarra flame tree)

The Illawarra flame tree is without doubt one of the most spectacular flowering trees in the world. The only problems are its relatively short flowering time and its unreliability of flowering from year to year. In its full glory, the leaves of the tree fall and are replaced by flowers on every part of the tree. There can, however, be a gap of several years between these stunning displays: in some years there may be no flowers and in others just part of the tree will flower. Generally, in cultivation it grows as a small to medium-sized tree, 10–20m in height, depending on the conditions. It comes from the rainforests of New South Wales and southern Queensland and so it will thrive in deep rich soil with plenty of water and compost added. If you want a bit of excitement in your gardening life, this is the tree for you as there is no more breathtaking sight in the botanical world than an Illawarra flame tree in full flower.

Brachyscome species and cultivars (native daisies)

These delightful little native daisies have really come of age in the last decade as plant collectors and breeders have dramatically increased the range available to gardeners. The low, mounding habit of the brachyscomes makes them ideal subjects for rockeries and the front of borders of shrubs and perennials. Their delicate daisy flowers blend wonderfully well with all sorts of plants, both Australian and exotic. In addition, they are very easy to propagate with tip-cuttings striking in a matter of weeks. Indeed, a number of *Brachyscome* species and cultivars will form roots underneath the dense mat of their growth and propagation is simply a matter of lifting the fringe of the plant, removing a rooted stem, and putting it in a pot to re-establish before replanting in the garden. Another option for some brachyscomes, such as *Brachyscome formosa* (often sold as 'Pilliga Posy') and *B.* 'Strawberry Mousse', that have a suckering habit is to propagate by dividing the clumps. A divided piece with a few shoots will happily establish a new clump within months.

For those confused over the spelling of brachy(s)come, it would appear that the botanists responsible for determining its spelling cannot agree: the Victorian botanists maintain that the correct spelling is brachyscome while their New South Wales counterparts insist that the 's' has to go. So if you're feeling a little confused by this situation then join the club! Whatever we choose to call them, there has been an explosion of interest in these plants from the nursery industry over the last 10 years. Various *Brachyscome* species have proved outstanding as garden plants, including *Brachyscome multifida* and its selected forms such as 'Amethyst' and 'Break O' Day', *B. angustifolia*, and *B. formosa* (often sold as 'Pilliga Posy').

In most cases the brachyscomes are perennial and groundcovering, growing into attractive clumps. Most brachyscomes have their flowering peak in spring, but some species will also flower sporadically throughout the year with major flushes through the warmer months. Many of the brachyscomes will flower all year round in frost-free climates. For details of flowering periods refer below to the listings of the various species and cultivars.

Brachyscome angustifolia
This species has been in cultivation for many years and comes from a range of climates but usually lives in boggy soil conditions. It is therefore happiest in moist soils in garden situations, preferably in full sun or light shade. It grows to a maximum height of 30cm and has a similar spread. It tends to have a fairly compact habit rather than spreading like other brachyscomes. The flowers are only about 2cm in size but they are produced in profusion throughout the warmer months, and the colour may be pink, blue or purple. It has been a parent to many interesting hybrids, which is a testimony to the adaptability and beauty of this lovely species.

Brachyscome formosa (often sold as 'Pilliga Posy')
This is a compact, groundcovering plant that suckers and spreads out to cover a large area. The leaves are 2–6cm long, 0.5–3.5cm wide, and have an interesting purplish underside. The flowers, each 2.5–3.5cm in size, are a stunning bright pink and borne on stalks held above the foliage. This species comes from inland New South Wales, which gives it the capacity to survive moderate frosts and drought. It has proved to be quite adaptable to a range of soil types and does well in either sun or semi-shade. The suckering habit of this plant makes it a natural for pot culture, rockeries, borders or hanging baskets. The purplish tinge to the foliage adds extra interest to this plant, giving it a rather different appearance to other brachyscomes.

Brachyscome iberidifolia (Swan River daisy)
This is a spectacular annual that was genetically improved in Europe last century. The varieties selected back then have survived to the current day and are available from seed merchants as 'Little Blue Star', 'Red Star' and 'Purple King'. It grows to about 30cm in height and has daisy flowers, each 2cm in size, in a variety of shades of white, blue-mauve or purple. One of the really attractive features of the Swan River daisy is that a percentage of the flowers have black centres, giving a great contrasting effect. The leaves are segmented and are about 3cm long. It is possible to buy seed in separate colours if desired. Seed should be sown in mid- to late winter for a spring flower display, and the normal garden conditions that one gives to exotic annuals will suit them just fine.

Brachyscome 'Just Jayne'
This cultivar is apparently a hybrid between *Brachyscome angustifolia* and a white-flowered selection of *B. multifida*, and it originated in Queensland. It has proved to be adaptable over a range of climates and soil types, and is at its best in full sun or light shade. It grows to a maximum height of 20cm and will spread to 1m wide under ideal conditions. The very pale lilac flowers are up to 3cm in size and are produced in profusion throughout the warmer months of the year.

Brachyscome 'Lemon Drops'
This is a more upright, spreading, perennial groundcover. It has small, fern-like divided leaves, up to 6cm long, and yellow flowers that are up to 2.3cm in size. The flower colour fades with age. It flowers from spring through into autumn. This cultivar performs well in subtropical climates such as that of Sydney. It has proved to be adaptable to a variety of soil types. The subsequently released cultivar *Brachyscome* 'Sunburst' (listed on page 47) appears to be at least as good, if not better, than *B.* 'Lemon Drops'.

The absolutely spectacular Illawarra flame tree (*Brachychiton acerifolius*) in its full glory

A mix of brachyscome cultivars that shows the range of colours available

Brachyscome 'Pink Haze', showing the typical growth habit of the brachyscome group

Swan River pea (*Brachysema lanceolata*)

Brachyscome multifida (cut-leaf daisy)
This is perhaps the best horticultural performer of the brachyscomes and has become incredibly popular in Europe and the United States as a windowbox or hanging basket plant, with hundreds of thousands of plants being sold annually in those continents. In fact, there is now even a German-bred cultivar on the market in Australia (the interestingly titled 'Toucan Tango'). The cut-leaf daisy has proved to be reliable and adaptable in all kinds of different soil types and climates. It will commonly grow about 10–30cm tall and as a groundcover can spread up to 1m wide. The flowers can be up to 2.5cm in size and come in white, pink, or pale to bright blue. It has attractive, mid-green, spidery foliage. A number of outstanding cultivars have been selected from the wild forms of *Brachyscome multifida* and these are detailed below.

Brachyscome multifida 'Amethyst'
This selection of *Brachyscome multifida* produces stunning violet-coloured flowers, each up to 2.5cm in size, for most of the year. It also has very pleasing, finely divided, ferny foliage and the stems often have a purplish tinge that brilliantly highlights the flowers. This cultivar is also reportedly tolerant of moderate frosts, the cooler weather actually producing attractive darker stems during the winter months.

Brachyscome multifida 'Blue Haze'
This compact, ground-hugging plant has leaves that are highly segmented, fleshy, dark green, and up to 2.5cm long. The large flowers, up to 3.5cm in size, are violet-blue with a golden centre and are borne throughout the warmer months. It is a great companion plant for *Brachyscome multifida* 'Pink Haze' (listed opposite) as it is very similar in form and style, and it can be used in similar situations. Like that cultivar, it is

capable of covering a fairly large area quickly. The unusual violet-blue colour of the flowers sets this cultivar apart and it is a very useful addition to any garden.

Brachyscome multifida 'Break O' Day'
This cultivar has proved to be an outstanding performer around the world. It is very reliable and has blue flowers, each about 2cm in size, with attractive yellow-green centres. The flowers are produced throughout the year. It self-layers as the plant spreads outward to a diameter of 1m or so. It has also proved to be moderately frost hardy and so will do well in climates like that of Canberra.

Brachyscome multifida var. *dilatata*
This is a wild form of the species that has broader leaf segments and slightly smaller, pale mauve-blue flowers. It has also proved to be hardy and floriferous over a range of soil and climate types.

Brachyscome multifida 'Pink Haze'
'Pink Haze' is a prostrate, compact perennial daisy with finely divided, dark green foliage. It produces pale pink flowers, each up to 2.5cm in size, all year round with peaks in the warm months. This is another outstanding groundcovering brachyscome that adapts well to a wide range of soil types and climates. This cultivar forms a small mound as it spreads laterally. It is hardy to light frosts as well. This is a fantastic plant for providing a low-maintenance groundcover on the edge of a bed. The pleasant flower colour blends well with almost anything. This cultivar is a very fast grower and with encouragement, by propagating more plants, you can cover a very large area with its wonderful pink haze.

Brachyscome 'Strawberry Mousse'
This plant is a hybrid between *Brachyscome angustifolia* and *B. formosa* (often sold as

'Pilliga Posy') and not surprisingly it has a very similar suckering growth habit to 'Pilliga Posy'. The leaves are about 2cm long and 0.5–1cm wide and are light green in colour. The pale pink daisy flowers are each up to 3.5cm in size and are borne on stalks held above the foliage. It flowers profusely from spring through to autumn. It is a very adaptable plant, flourishes in a range of soil types, and does well in sun or semi-shade. It is proving to be a very good seller overseas and is one of the most popular Australian plants on the market in Europe and the United States.

Brachyscome 'Sunburst'
This is a compact, perennial groundcovering plant that has a somewhat upright habit. It has small leaves, 2.5–3cm long, that have a toothed margin, and yellow flowers that are up to 2.5cm in size and on stems about 15cm tall. The flower colour fades with age. It blooms throughout the year with a spectacular flush in spring. This cultivar has proved to be reliable over a range of climates and soil types. It does have a tendency to become a little bit leggy in cultivation, but a light trim of about 20 per cent after a large flush of flowers will keep the plant looking its best. 'Sunburst' is well worth a try as a border plant in any sort of garden, native or exotic.

Brachyscome 'Valencia'
This cultivar grows as a tight clump and is about 20cm in height to the flower tops. The segmented, mid-green leaves are about 5cm long. It has pale pink flowers that are relatively large, 5cm in size, and well displayed above the foliage. It flowers all year round with a peak in the warmer months. It prefers moist, well-drained soils and full sun or light shade. A light trim after a heavy flush of flowers will help to encourage the next flush. This has proved to be a very popular cultivar as evidenced by

how well it sells in nurseries. It is a good choice for rockeries, hanging baskets or garden borders.

Brachysema lanceolata (Swan River pea)
The Swan River pea is a particularly versatile winter-flowering plant. It has rather large, red pea flowers that supply nectar to honey-eating birds, and the dark green foliage has a gorgeous silver underside that creates an interesting effect in the garden. It can spread up to 3m in diameter and can therefore be used as a groundcover, but it also has the ability to climb and create a screen if this is your requirement. It has proved to be adaptable to a wide range of soil and climatic conditions and will tolerate moderate frosts. There is also a number of other interesting *Brachysema* species that have similar qualities to *Brachysema lanceolata* and are well worth growing.

Bracteantha species and cultivars (strawflowers)
The daisy family (Asteraceae) is arguably the most successful and widespread group of flowering plants in the world. Daisies can be found in profusion from deserts to alpine areas, from windswept coastal headlands to the edges of waterfalls. Every continent has its own unique group of daisy species and Australia is no exception with its fascinating paper daisies and strawflowers.

The strawflower (*Bracteantha bracteata*) is one of our most colourful and adaptable native plants and it can be used to great effect in the garden. These are rather remarkable plants that can provide interesting flower colour and texture. In fact, horticulturists in Europe in the 1800s recognised the potential in several different types and spent many years breeding superior new varieties. The strawflowers (then known as *Helichrysum bracteatum* but recently reclassified by botanists as

Strawflower (*Bracteantha bracteata*) can provide spectacular colour for many months of the year

Ivory curl (*Buckinghamia celsissima*) is ideal for subtropical and warm temperature climates

The incense plant (*Calomeria amaranthoides*) is an unusual member of the daisy family

The fiery red of *Callistemon citrinus* is typical of this genus

Callistemon 'Candy Pink'

Bracteantha bracteata) were the subject of an intensive breeding program in Germany. The end result of this was an incredible array of colours, shapes and sizes that are still popular to this day. Seed of these strains is readily available from nurseries and supermarkets. The larger-flowered types are sometimes sold as *Helichrysum* 'Monstrosum', while a much more compact type that grows to less than 50cm in height is sold as *H.* 'Bright Bikini'. They will provide excellent colour through spring and summer.

Various perennial forms of *Bracteantha bracteata* have become increasingly popular in the last 10 years or so. In many ways, the new cultivars could be thought of as occupying a similar position in the native garden as marguerite daisies do in the exotic or cottage garden. In other words, they can be compact mounds of colour that are at their best for a couple of years. Tip-pruning while they are young and deadheading of the spent flowers will bring wonderful rewards in shaping the plants into a compact habit (see section on pruning, pages 22–23). Like marguerite daisies, the perennial strawflowers will look best if you consider their useful life span to be 2–3 years. It is best to then renew your plants from tip-cuttings taken in the warmer months of the year. These perennial cultivars strike very easily from soft tip-cuttings and behave in a very similar way to the exotic marguerite daisies. They benefit greatly from regular removal of the dead flowers and will self seed if allowed to.

Bracteantha bracteata 'Cockatoo'
This cultivar is very similar to 'Dargan Hill Monarch' (listed next) except that it has exquisite, lemon yellow flower heads that are slightly smaller than those of 'Dargan Hill Monarch'. The delicate lemon yellow colour is very attractive. This cultivar has proved to be very adaptable and long-lived in garden situations.

Bracteantha bracteata 'Dargan Hill Monarch'
This beautiful cultivar forms a bushy mounded plant that grows to about 1m high and wide. It has attractive, greyish green furry leaves and produces golden yellow flower heads, each up to 10cm in size, over a long period through the warmer months of the year. One of the most reliable of the *Bracteantha* cultivars, it is also one of the more compact ones, although tip-pruning will give an even better result. This colourful plant will provide a great display reminiscent of an annual flowerbed.

Bracteantha bracteata 'Diamond Head'
In contrast to the other cultivars described, this one is a groundcover about 20cm high and 50cm wide. It was originally selected from a low-growing coastal population of this species growing near Diamond Head on the New South Wales north coast. It has small, narrow, bright green foliage and produces masses of smallish yellow flower heads that have orange centres. It flowers throughout the warmer months of the year and is absolutely ideal for rockeries or pot culture and also likes full sun. Being from a coastal situation, it will also tolerate wind and salt spray to some extent. Like 'Dargan Hill Monarch', it is not a long-lived plant and should be replaced with new cuttings when it starts to become open in growth and flowering slows down. A similar cultivar that is worth looking for is *Bracteantha bracteata* 'Hastings Gold', which has a similar growth habit but larger flowers up to 5cm in size.

Bracteantha bracteata 'Golden Bowerbird'
This cultivar is similar to 'Dargan Hill Monarch' in plant habit but it has flowers that are much fuller and larger and the leaves are not quite as grey in colour. Like 'Dargan Hill Monarch', it is also an outstandingly free-flowering plant.

Bracteantha bracteata 'White Monarch'
This cultivar is also rather similar to 'Dargan Hill Monarch' except that the flower heads are a beautiful, clean white colour with orange centres and are up to 8cm in size. The leaves are not quite as grey in colour as those of 'Dargan Hill Monarch'. This plant brings a nice fresh tinge of colour to the garden and makes an ideal companion to 'Dargan Hill Monarch'.

Buckinghamia celsissima (ivory curl)

This showy member of the Proteaceae family is wonderful for warmer climates such as Sydney and Brisbane. It can grow up to 2m tall by 1m or more wide, and becomes absolutely covered in ivory-coloured, brush-shaped flowers in early summer when there is not much else in flower in the garden. Unlike many members of this family, it is not particularly sensitive to phosphorus and will fit quite comfortably into an exotic garden as its glossy foliage is an ideal foil for plants such as camellias and gardenias. It flowers best in full sun and is best grown in a well-drained loamy soil that retains reasonable amounts of moisture. It is not tolerant of frosts at all, unfortunately. The soft creamy colour of the flowers blends well with a wide range of other flower colours in the garden.

Callicarpa pedunculata

Unfortunately, this rather exotic-looking rainforest plant from northern New South Wales is rarely seen in nurseries; it is, nevertheless, well worth tracking down. Grow it for its soft green, velvety leaves and spectacular clusters of purple berry fruits that are prominent up and down the stems in late spring and early summer. The plant can grow up to 2m in height and width, and responds well to pruning after the fruits have dropped. It is not particularly frost hardy but will thrive in a warmer climate on a loamy soil and also responds well to general purpose slow-release or other fertiliser.

Callicoma serratifolia (blackwattle)

This small, bushy tree is a common inhabitant of rainforests along the New South Wales and Queensland coast. The shiny, dark green leaves are a feature that makes this a great background screen plant. The foliage also has an interesting rusty underside and the saw-toothed edge of the leaf gives the plant an attractive textural quality. In spring, the fluffy, pale yellow, powder puff flowers are prominent as an added bonus. It is tolerant of mild frosts but will thrive best in a warmer climate on a loamy soil and also responds well to general purpose slow-release or other fertiliser.

Callistemon species and cultivars (bottlebrushes)

The bottlebrush genus represents one of the most adaptable and useful groups of plants in the Australian flora. There are approximately 25 species and most come from habitats such as river banks and creek banks where they are usually growing in soil that is periodically waterlogged, or rather moist at other times, while during drought it can be completely dry. Consequently, most bottlebrushes will thrive in wet or dry conditions, from sandy soils to heavy clays.

As far as flower colour goes, red is most commonly associated with bottlebrushes, but you may be pleasantly surprised to discover some of the subtle pink and mauve hues that are available, as well as pure whites and yellows.

Bottlebrushes range from large trees, such as *Callistemon salignus,* to shrubs of all sizes, down to the miniature shrub *C.* 'Little John'. They make excellent screen or hedge plants as they respond very well to pruning.

The New South Wales Christmas bush provides a brilliant summer display

The care of bottlebrushes is straightforward. For the best flowering performance, select a site that gets as much sunlight as possible. Bottlebrushes will survive quite well in shady conditions but do not expect peak flowering. Generally speaking, flowering of most species and cultivars is in the spring but there are many that will flower on and off through summer and autumn, as detailed on the following pages. Accordingly, when pruning your bottlebrush, simply cut off the spent flowers just below the stem. If this is done in spring, it will result in increased branching which means more flowers, and indeed such pruning may even encourage a burst of flowering later in summer and autumn.

One word of caution with bottlebrushes in the garden—they love moisture and tend to seek out underground water and drain

New South Wales Christmas bush (*Ceratopetalum gummiferum*)

Geraldton wax (*Chamelaucium uncinatum*) has been a spectacular success worldwide both as a cut flower and garden plant

pipes. So be careful where you plant them in your garden to avoid any nasty surprises later. Below is a list of the various bottlebrush species and cultivars (sorted by colour) commonly available through the nursery trade.

Red

The majority of bottlebrush species are red flowered. A few of the outstanding species are described below but it is worth emphasising that most of the species not listed here have made excellent garden plants and can all be recommended. Local species, if there are any, will be the best for any given area of Australia.

Callistemon citrinus (lemon-scented bottlebrush, scarlet bottlebrush)
This species has long been popular in cultivation and has been the parent for quite a few cultivars such as 'King's Park Special' (listed below) and 'Western Glory'. When *Callistemon citrinus* is grown from seed, it can vary from 2m to 8m tall and from 2m to 6m wide; however, more vigorous types can be pruned into a more compact shape. The flower spike can be up to 12cm long and 6cm wide and is among the most spectacular of the bottlebrushes.

Callistemon citrinus 'Endeavour'
This cultivar is a selection of *Callistemon citrinus* that has stood the test of time, having originally been released back in 1970 to commemorate Captain Cook's 'discovery' of the Australian east coast in his ship the *Endeavour*. It has dark green, dense, stiff foliage and can grow to a height and width of around 4m. It produces large crimson flower spikes, up to 12cm long, virtually all year round in warmer climates. The compact nature of this form makes it an excellent hedge or screen plant. It also tolerates frost and coastal exposure reasonably well.

Callistemon salignus 'Great Balls of Fire'
This compact shrub produces many more branches than the typical *Callistemon salignus* and has medium-sized lance-shaped leaves. The fiery red new growth it produces throughout spring gives it its cultivar name. This foliage colour is the main reason for growing this cultivar and a small dose of native plant fertiliser every month or so during the warmer months will encourage more of the colourful new growth. The cream-coloured flowers are not a prominent feature of the plant but they do add interest in late spring. A light prune after flowering will help to keep this plant as a very compact bun-shaped shrub. It makes a wonderful contrast plant in the garden.

Callistemon viminalis (weeping bottlebrush)
This is an extremely variable species that is the parent of many interesting cultivars such as 'Captain Cook', 'Dawson River', 'Hannah Ray', 'Little John' and 'Rose Opal', some of which are listed in the following entries. It can grow from 1m to 12m tall and from 1m to 5m wide. The flowers may be from 5cm to 20cm long and from 3cm to 6cm wide. The foliage is covered in soft, silky hairs that provide an interesting textural element for the garden, particularly when there is new growth tinged with pink or red. The species is worth growing from seed; however, if you want a more predictable result, then go for one of the *Callistemon viminalis* cultivars listed here.

Callistemon viminalis 'Captain Cook'
This bottlebrush was released around 1970 as a sister plant to 'Endeavour' (listed above) and is a dwarf, rounded shrub to 2m tall, with small, soft, slightly weeping foliage. It has bright red brushes in clusters near the ends of the branches, mainly in spring but some flowers generally appear throughout the warmer months. This is a compact selection of an outstanding species. It has

proved to be very adaptable and hardy and is an excellent choice for a smallish, spectacular red-flowering shrub.

Callistemon viminalis 'Hannah Ray'
Another selection of the weeping bottlebrush, this cultivar forms a small tree that is 5m tall by 2–3m wide. The pendulous foliage is covered in soft hairs and the new growth has a distinct, bright pink tinge to it in early spring. It has masses of pendulous, bright crimson brushes toward the end of spring and then again in autumn. This is a rather tall bottlebrush and should be given plenty of room to reach its full potential as an excellent screen plant. It benefits greatly from pruning back of the old flowers when the flush has finished.

Callistemon 'King's Park Special'
This outstanding bottlebrush forms a large upright shrub, 3–4m tall and 2–3m wide, with attractive, dense foliage. Its bright red flower spikes, about 10cm long, are borne throughout spring and summer. It arose as a seedling at the King's Park Botanic Gardens in Perth and is probably a hybrid between *Callistemon viminalis* and *C. citrinus*, combining the best features of both of these popular species. It has proved to be very adaptable to different soil and climatic conditions and is a perfect choice for a screen, hedge or background plant in difficult soil conditions such as heavy clays. If you were to grow only one bottlebrush in your garden, this would be a great choice.

Callistemon 'Little John'
This interesting cultivar is a dwarf shrub, 0.5–1m tall by up to 1m wide. The foliage is a feature as it has a pleasant bluish tinge to it and this makes a lovely contrast with the fiery red flower spikes that are up to 5cm long. Flowering rarely reaches a crescendo, but does occur throughout the warmer months, and the plant's compactness and

unusual foliage also make up for this. It is perhaps the smallest of all the *Callistemon* cultivars and looks attractive at all times in the garden. Another useful aspect of this plant is that it does not set seed, and, because there are no seed pods, there is no real need to prune it after flowering unless you want an extremely compact plant. It is therefore the ultimate low-maintenance plant.

Pink and mauve
Pinks and mauves are not common in flowers of this genus but are nonetheless a welcome addition to the gardener's colour palette.

Callistemon 'Candy Pink'
This subtly coloured bottlebrush grows into a medium-sized shrub, 4m tall by 1–3m wide, with stiff, bright green foliage. The flower spikes are up to 15cm long and are a lovely pink colour when first open before aging to an even darker pink. The flowers are borne in flushes virtually all year round, especially in warmer climates. This is a very reliable pink-flowered bottlebrush as it adapts well to different soil types and will withstand waterlogging and frost. A light pruning after flowering, followed by a handful of slow-release native plant food, will encourage the next flush of flowers.

Callistemon 'Mauve Mist'
'Mauve Mist' is an excellent name for this cultivar with its unusual and beautiful flower colour. It has been in cultivation for many decades and has stood the test of time. It is a dense shrub growing to 3m high by 3m wide, with fairly stiff leaves that are about 50mm long and about 8mm wide and have an interesting texture due to the silky hairs that are a feature of the new growth. It produces a fantastic display of 7cm-long mauve brushes during spring and will have smaller flushes at other times. It makes an

The white-flowered *Clematis aristata* is delightful in spring

exceptional screen or hedge plant and adapts well to different soil and climate types.

Callistemon 'Pink Alma'
This is a somewhat open shrub that grows 2–3m high by 1m wide. Its leaves are fairly stiff and about 70mm long by about 15mm wide. It is smothered in bright pink brushes (70mm by 50mm in size) throughout winter and spring and sporadically at other times of the year. This relatively new cultivar has beautifully coloured flowers and a vigorous growth habit. It does particularly well in the Sydney region.

White
White-flowering bottlebrush can be used to create interesting contrasts in your garden.

Callistemon 'White Anzac' (sometimes sold as *C.* 'Anzac')
This cultivar is something of a novelty for

Crowea exalata provides a welcome splash of pink in autumn

Dampiera 'Glasshouse Glory'

Darwinia oxylepis is a spectacular plant that is best grown in pots to ensure perfect drainage

the bottlebrush group with its unusual white flower spikes. It is a rather open shrub that reaches not much more than 1m high and grows up to 2m wide. The leaves are fairly stiff and up to 60mm long by about 10mm wide. It has large, white brushes with a tinge of pink throughout the summer months. It has proved to be adaptable over a wide range of climates and soils. Its tendency to develop an open, ungainly habit can be overcome by regular tip-pruning in the first year or two after planting and then give it a light prune after each flush of flowers.

Yellow
The subtle lemon tones of the following bottlebrushes can be very uplifting in a colour scheme.

Callistemon pallidus (lemon bottlebrush)
This lovely species grows up to 5m tall by 2–5m wide and produces its attractive lemon yellow brushes from spring to early summer. Each flower head is up to 10cm long and they are produced in profusion. The plant is tolerant of frost, wind, waterlogging and coastal exposure. It makes a good screen, hedge or windbreak.

Callistemon salignus (willow bottlebrush)
Not a plant for the smaller garden, the willow bottlebrush can grow into a small to medium-sized tree that is up to 15m tall by 5m wide. The flower heads are relatively small at 5cm long by 2–3cm wide and are produced throughout spring. Flower colour in this species varies from the normal creamy white through to pink, red or mauve. It is a frost hardy species that adapts well to different soils and makes a very useful street tree or larger screen plant. One last word of advice: do not plant it near underground pipes or drains.

Calocephalus (syn. *Leucophyta*) *brownii* (cushion bush)
This lovely little member of the daisy family (Asteraceae) lives up to its common name because it grows into a 50cm ball. It is a fantastic foliage plant with its dense habit and soft, downy, silvery green leaves. In summer, the foliage is complemented by small, creamy yellow flowers. The natural habitat of this plant is on the coastal frontline where it is blasted by wind and salt, so it will adapt well to most garden stresses. It can withstand mild frost and has proved to be adaptable to most soil types. This is the perfect border plant if you want to establish a white or silver garden.

Calomeria amaranthoides (incense plant)
The daisy family (Asteraceae) is not normally associated with perfume but there is a very unusual Australian member of this family which goes by the appropriate name of incense plant. Thousands of minute daisy flowers are borne in flowing reddish bronze plumes on a 2m-high stem. The flower head is actually much more reminiscent of a grass, so tiny are the individual daisy flowers. The aroma of the flowers can be detected from several metres away and is retained when the flowers are dried (simply leave the cut stems in a dry vase).

This species has a very interesting history as it was grown in large pots in England in the 19th century for the purpose of placing in ballrooms for gala occasions because its perfume reputedly acted as an aphrodisiac. This is certainly something to watch out for if you are growing it in your garden and some unsuspecting member of the appropriate sex strolls by! The plant is not commonly available in the nursery trade, however, seeds are sometimes available through the Australian Plant Society. It is a biennial plant, forming a rosette of leaves after the seed is planted in the autumn.

Eighteen months later the tall flower stems are produced. It requires a well-drained soil and full sun to reach its full potential.

Ceratopetalum species and cultivars

The ceratopetalums have wonderful glossy green foliage to complement their red or pink flowers.

Ceratopetalum apetalum (coachwood)
The coachwood is an adaptable and majestic rainforest tree that grows in favourable situations along the east coast of Australia in New South Wales and Queensland. Its best features from a gardener's point of view are, firstly, the subtly beautiful trunk that develops as the tree ages and, secondly, a lovely display of flowers in early summer. It needs plenty of room and a fairly deep soil, as it can grow to 20m or more. Like its cousin the New South Wales Christmas bush (*Ceratopetalum gummiferum*), it develops a spectacular display of pink or red flowers around Christmas time. It can tolerate light frosts and becomes even more resistant as it increases in height. Give it plenty of water and fertiliser for best results.

Ceratopetalum gummiferum (New South Wales Christmas bush)
The New South Wales Christmas bush is a spectacular plant that has long been sold as a cut flower at Christmas time in the Sydney region. It should be noted that in southern States, such as Victoria and South Australia, it produces its colourful display in January rather than December. In the wild this plant prefers creek banks on humus-enriched alluvial sands, so it is no surprise that such soil conditions will give the best results in the garden. Indeed, planting on poorly drained soils seems to make it much more susceptible to fungal root rot and often leads to disappointment.

The rich, dark green foliage of New South Wales Christmas bush makes it an attractive background plant in the garden, and indeed florists use it as backing foliage in their arrangements. During late spring the true flowers, which are actually white, are produced. As spring turns to early summer, the petals drop off and the sepals that surround them start to enlarge and change colour to create the fiery red display that gardeners are so familiar with.

For the best results with flowering, it is important not to fertilise the plants in spring because feeding will result in lots of vegetative 'bypass' growth that will then hide the flowers. Instead it is best to prune the plants lightly after flowering and then fertilise with a couple of handfuls of slow-release native plant food followed by a thorough watering. This will produce a framework of vegetative growth that will give you profuse flowering in the next season. New South Wales Christmas bush can be pruned much harder if you are trying to renovate an old neglected tree. It can be pruned as hard as you like, back to the stump if necessary, but be aware that this will probably result in very few, if any, flowers in the following season.

Ceratopetalum gummiferum 'Albery's Red'
This cultivar is probably the best of all the New South Wales Christmas bush selections so far. It has a compact form and grows to about 5m tall. The glossy green foliage is spectacularly complemented with a brilliant, very bright red, floral display fairly early in the season (before Christmas in Sydney). This cultivar will provide ample flowers for both the garden and for cutting. It is very reliable and makes a great feature plant in any garden bed with full sun.

Ceratopetalum gummiferum 'Magenta Star'
This is a very vigorous selection of New South Wales Christmas bush that features beautiful magenta-coloured new growth

Hardenbergia species, a lovely touch of blue

throughout spring and summer. The rapidly growing shoot tips have the strongest colour and as they grow the foliage and stems gradually fade to green. The new foliage can be used as a feature in early spring and is followed by a good display of red flowers at Christmas. This cultivar may be a little hard to find, but it is worth the effort as it will bring colour to your garden throughout spring and summer.

Ceratopetalum gummiferum 'Mirrabooka'
This is a white-flowered form of this versatile shrub, selected by native plant enthusiasts Jeremy and Martin Smith. It is a vigorous form that grows to 5m or more, with rather striking, light green foliage and yellowish stems. Like all New South Wales Christmas bushes, it can be ruthlessly pruned if the need arises.

Chamelaucium species and cultivars (Geraldton wax)

Geraldton wax (so called because it is indigenous to the area around Geraldton, Western Australia) has been one of the great success stories of Australian plants worldwide due to its exceptional qualities as a cut flower. Various forms of Geraldton wax are widely grown in such diverse places as Israel, California and Italy. It is also gaining in popularity as a pot plant because it can be made to flower at any time of year by commercial growers (who do this by manipulating the daylength the plant receives, thus triggering flowering).

Geraldton wax has proved to be a rather adaptable plant in cultivation, however golden rules are that it requires very good drainage and full sun to reach its full potential. Under ideal conditions, it can

The striking flower head of the Gymea lily (*Doryanthes excelsa*) will attract many different birds to your garden

grow to 2–3m in height by a similar width. If this sounds a little big for your backyard, then have no fear, as it can be pruned to whatever size and shape you require and this is best done straight after the plant finishes flowering in springtime. An alternative is to prune the plant by cutting the flowers for indoor use or for giving away to friends and loved ones.

Another important point in growing Geraldton wax is to withhold fertiliser and water in the few months before they flower in early spring. The problem with fertilising near flowering time is that it produces a vigorous burst of vegetative growth that will hide your flowers. It is best to fertilise after you have trimmed back the plant by 20 to 30 per cent after flowering. A couple of handfuls of slow-release fertiliser at this time will be richly rewarded.

The most common Geraldton wax in cultivation is the natural pink form of *Chamelaucium uncinatum*. There are also many cultivars of Geraldton wax available.

Chamelaucium uncinatum 'Purple Pride'
This cultivar has been perhaps the most successful selection of Geraldton wax. It has spectacular displays of reddish purple flowers from early to mid-spring. In all other respects, it conforms to the above description and culture of Geraldton wax.

Chlorocephalum apiculatum (syn. *Helichrysum apiculatum*)

This very versatile and hardy member of the everlasting daisy group occurs in all States of Australia. It is a dwarf perennial plant that makes a superb groundcover. There are a number of different forms in cultivation but none grows taller than 50cm and they will all potentially spread into a ball-shape that is up to 2m wide. It is widespread in the eastern States of Australia and comes in a number of forms, some more compact than others. The different forms also vary widely in their

foliage colour, from light green to perhaps the more desirable silvery grey, which is the form most commonly offered for sale. The plant has proved to be adaptable to frost and tolerates most soil types provided that the drainage is at least moderate. This is a superb choice as a groundcover or pot plant and it also makes a good cut flower.

Chorizema cordatum (flame pea)

The most common flame pea in cultivation is *Chorizema cordatum*—its iridescent pink and orange flowers will bring an unusually vibrant dash of colour to your garden. It comes from the relatively high rainfall area of the southwestern tip of Western Australia and this seems to make it a lot more adaptable to the average garden conditions found in many parts of Australia. It is a relatively easy plant to grow if given a moderately well-drained soil and light shade or full sun. If given support, such as a trellis, it will climb but otherwise it will form a small shrub that reaches no more than 1m in height. It flowers over a period of a couple of months during spring. A light pruning after flowering will help to keep it compact. This plant is an exceptionally good one for containers.

Cissus species (native grapes)

A species common to the rainforests of southeastern Australia is the water vine or native grape (*Cissus antarctica*). This member of the grape family (Vitaceae) is, like its cousin the common grape, a vigorous climber that can tolerate full sun or shade without any trouble. If there are no means of support handy, it can form a groundcover that will be impenetrable to weeds. It is capable of spreading to a width of many metres and the glossy leaves make a wonderful soft carpet, particularly in a shady, rainforest type of garden. The dark-coloured fruits are produced in summer and, while they look rather grape-like, they taste terrible.

In spite of this, rainforest birds such as the topknot pigeon seem to find them irresistible. Also worth mentioning is the five-leaf water vine (*Cissus hypoglauca*) which has a similar growth habit to its close relative but has an attractive five-fingered leaf, as its common name suggests. Both species are frost tender and prefer moist conditions for best results.

Clematis aristata (goat's beard)

This vigorous climber is found in moist gullies along the entire east coast of Australia, a testimony to its hardiness and adaptability. It grows to whatever degree of support it is given and will also make a nice groundcover if unsupported. It produces a spectacular display of white starry flowers in spring, followed by the subtle beauty of the fruits which form feathery clusters that persist on the plant into summer. The foliage is also interesting, being three fingered and having a mauve-coloured reverse that is an additional decorative feature of this plant. It grows well in most soil types provided the drainage is moderate and it will withstand most frosts.

Conostylis species (cotton heads)

Conostylis is a very interesting genus of plants from Western Australia. They are a close relative of the kangaroo paws and share the same hairiness on the flowers. In fact, the hairs on the flowers actually provide the yellow or orange pigments that give them their colour. Unlike the kangaroo paws, however, the *Conostylis* have their flowers bunched together in a globular head at the end of the usually compact flower stems. This gives the flower head the appearance of a yellow drumstick.

The plants form a tufty sort of clump that is much smaller than that of most kangaroo paws. Generally, the various *Conostylis* species like a well-drained situation and resent high humidity. However, in humid areas, it is possible to grow them as pot plants or rockery specimens and it is also useful to mulch around them with gravel rather than organic materials. The most reliable *Conostylis* species in cultivation are *Conostylis candicans*, with flowers held on stems that are 40–60cm long, and *C. seorsiflora*, a fascinating groundcover that holds its hairy tubular flowers down among the foliage at ground level.

Correa species and cultivars

The correas belong to the citrus family (Rutaceae) and their closest native relatives include the boronias and eriostemons. They are much hardier than either of these two groups in the garden and, as a bonus, many of them flower mainly in winter. Correas generally prefer a lightly shaded position, such as under eucalypts, and are adaptable to most soil types provided the drainage is good. They are generally a low-maintenance type of plant. Most species and cultivars are reasonably frost tolerant, and respond well to a light pruning all over after flowering.

Correa alba (white correa)
This is a fabulous plant for those interested in creating white or silver gardens. It grows to a height and width of about 1m. The foliage is covered in soft, white hairs that give the plant a silvery tinge. Another feature is the plant's great adaptability, something that derives from its natural habitat which is usually very close to the ocean. It will happily withstand wind, salt and a range of soil types. The white starry flowers are scattered through the foliage in spring. White correa is one of the hardiest native plants for your garden and will also thrive in inland areas.

Correa baeuerlenii (chef's cap correa)
This is one for the gardener who is looking for something out of the ordinary. The unusual, green tubular flowers have a very distinctive 'chef's cap' at the top that is formed from a flattened calyx. It is a fairly

rare species in the wild and that is another good reason to grow it in our gardens. Growing to a height and width of about 2m, it can be pruned to whatever shape you desire and makes an excellent small hedge. The foliage is a rich, dark green that will add interest to the garden all year round.

Correa 'Dusky Bells'
This is a dwarf shrub that tends to have a groundcovering habit, growing to 1m tall by up to 2m wide. The smallish leaves are covered in star-shaped hairs when they are young. It bears subtle pink, tubular flowers, 4cm long by 1cm wide, through the cooler months of the year when there is generally a scarcity of flowers in the garden. Like all correas, it is quite attractive to honey-eating birds. Its groundcovering habit tends to smother weeds.

Correa 'Marion's Marvel'
This is a small shrub that will grow to about 2m tall and wide. The leaves are dark green

and smallish. The tubular flowers are an interesting mix of pink at the base tipped with green. The flowers are borne from late summer through to the end of winter. This is a more upright plant than 'Dusky Bells' (listed above) and is quite useful for screen plantings or even as a feature plant. Its subtle flower colour will appeal to anyone who is wanting to bring pastel shades into their garden colour scheme.

Correa reflexa (common correa)
Probably the most common species in the wild, the common correa is found near the coastline of every State of Australia. Typically it grows as a shrub 1–2m in height and width, but there are groundcovering forms as well. The tubular flowers are usually about 3cm long and are red tipped with green, although there are numerous colour forms that include cream and pink as well. This great coastal correa has its peak flowering in winter but often produces a few flowers at other times of the year.

Blueberry ash (*Elacocarpus reticulatus* 'Prima Donna')

Pink waxflower (*Eriostemon australasius*)

The wonderful hardy *Philotheca* syn. *Eriostemon myoporoides*

Crowea species and cultivars

The croweas also belong to the citrus family (Rutaceae) and generally have gorgeous, starry pink flowers. One of their great virtues is that they are generally autumn flowering and the display continues for an extended period, usually over several months. They are, it has to be said, not the most reliable plants in the garden and are best grown as pot plants where their need for good drainage can be catered for easily. A light pruning after flowering and a handful of slow-release fertiliser in spring is the only maintenance required to keep them looking good. As a group, they do best in well-drained soils and lightly shaded situations.

Crowea exalata, C. saligna, C. angustifolia and *C.* 'Festival' are all worth growing and will all reach about 1–2m in height and width. The croweas produce pink flowers in autumn, with the exception of the spring-flowering *C. angustifolia*. If you are looking for a more compact dwarf form with similar attributes, then try and find a cultivar called 'Bindelong Compact' which has a reputation for being the hardiest of the croweas currently in cultivation.

Dampiera species and cultivars

If you are looking to provide a royal blue flower for your garden, then dampieras are the plants for you. Named after the famous 17th-century explorer William Dampier, there are some 66 species that occur in the wild and only in Australia. Most species are either low-growing or even prostrate groundcovers that can be used in containers or look fantastic spilling over rockeries or garden beds. Blue is an uncommon flower colour at the best of times, so the royal blues and purples of the dampieras are a godsend to Australian gardeners.

The dampieras are widely distributed around Australia, with many species in Western Australia. There are not as many species in the eastern States but those that are there, such as *Dampiera stricta* and *D. purpurea,* have proved to be reasonably reliable in cultivation, particularly as potted plants. In the wild, dampieras generally inhabit soils with very good drainage and they grow in open areas such as heathlands where they are in full sun. Given such conditions in the garden, they will be right at home. The plants generally grow from a fleshy rootstock and the best way to regenerate them is to give them a light trim after a flush of flowers. Perhaps the most realistic way to look at dampieras, however, is as annual plants that will give a brilliant display for many months but may not survive to a second season.

Dampiera diversifolia

This species has established itself as a long-flowering garden plant that will tolerate a fairly wide range of conditions. It has the most vivid purple-blue flowers imaginable. Another advantage of this plant is its ability to sucker from the roots. This means it will spread as a groundcover up to 1m in width. It needs a well-drained soil, full sun and protection from heavy frosts.

Darwinia species

There are many very spectacular species of *Darwinia*, particularly from Western Australia, but most have proved to be difficult to cultivate in garden situations. So they are perhaps best left to the Australian plant enthusiasts who are prepared to give them the tender loving care which they need to flourish. There is, however, one species that can be recommended.

Darwinia citriodora (lemon-scented myrtle)

This dwarf shrub grows up to a couple of metres high and wide and it has delightfully perfumed, grey-green leaves that alone make it worthy of a place in the garden. In spring, an added bonus is the orange-red flowers that are dotted through the foliage. This species has proved itself to be very hardy to frost and coastal conditions. It requires reasonably well-drained soil and thrives in full sun or light shade.

Dendrobium speciosum (rock orchid)

The rock orchid lights up the spring garden with its long and spectacular sprays of creamy white flowers that have an interesting and pleasant perfume. Orchids generally have a reputation as being difficult to grow and needing lots of attention, but this is definitely an exception as it will happily grow outdoors in a wide range of climatic conditions, from subtropical to temperate. It grows naturally from northeastern Queensland to eastern Victoria, in a wide variety of habitats from rainforest to dry sandstone outcrops in eucalypt forests. Clumps will gradually increase in size and will eventually expand to several metres in diameter if space allows. A high light situation will give best flowering, but even full sun will be happily tolerated by this tough orchid. Ideally, it loves to grow on sandstone rock ledges but it can also be readily grown in pots in a suitable coarse medium that is recommended for orchids. The growth period extends through the warmer months of spring and summer and the plants should be given lots of water and regular liquid fertiliser during this period if the best flowering is to be obtained.

Dianella species (native flax lilies)

This interesting group of clumping perennials deserves greater attention in the garden. All the *Dianella* species in cultivation are compact, growing to less than 1m in height, and all feature lovely sprays of blue flowers that are followed by masses of fleshy berries that vary in colour from purple to blue. They generally come from reasonably moist environments along the edges of creeks and forests. They have

proved to be fairly adaptable to a range of drainage conditions and soil types, and do best in lightly shaded situations, such as under eucalypts. Undoubtedly the hardiest is *Dianella revoluta*, but other species to look out for include *D. tasmanica* and *D. caerulea*.

Doryanthes species (spear lilies)

The distinctive, large, strappy, light green leaves of the giant spear lily have captured the attention of garden designers in recent years. The foliage is so spectacular that it is reason enough to include this plant in your garden. The long, spear-like flowers are an added bonus when they appear in springtime. Be prepared to see them as a bonus though, as it can take many years for the spear lily to flower from seed and there is no guarantee that it will flower every year once it has started.

They are seemingly indestructible plants that will survive all kinds of abuse, even accidental poisoning with herbicides such as glyphosate. They will, however, give best results if planted in a deep, fertile, loamy soil, where they will grow to very large proportions with the entire clump having the potential to reach several metres in diameter. The foliage a can grow to 2m tall. The flower stems can grow to 10m tall but may be only about 2m in height at the first flowering.

There are only two species of *Doryanthes* but both are available and are easy to grow in most areas of Australia. With some frost protection in the first couple of years when they are establishing, they can even be grown in climates as cold as that of Canberra. *Doryanthes excelsa* (Gymea lily) is the frost hardier of the two species and has a clump of leathery flowers atop a stem that can be 1–10m tall.

The other species, *Doryanthes palmeri* (spear lily), comes from the New South Wales north coast, from places such as the slopes of Mount Warning; however, it is

Gungurru (*Eucalyptus caesia*) needs a climate with dry summers if it is to thrive

Eucalyptus leucoxylon subs. *megalocarpa* adapts well to east-coast garden conditions

Eucalyptus syn. *Corymbia ficifolia* is an orange-coloured form of the red flowering gum

successfully cultivated as far south as Melbourne. It also has fiery red flowers but instead of being in a terminal cluster, they are spread out in toothbrush fashion at the top of the flower stems that can reach up to 4–5m in height.

Elaeocarpus reticulatus (blueberry ash)

The blueberry ash will need no introduction to many gardeners. While its preferred habitat is around the margins of rainforests, it can often be found toughing it out with the eucalypts and banksias in the dry sclerophyll forests of eastern Australia. It will, however, respond to well-watered and fertilised soil conditions. Its delicate, lacy, bell-shaped flowers have given rise to the alternative common name of lily-of-the-valley tree and the showy display of flowers is followed by bright blue fruits that are held on the plant into winter. Its natural distribution is from southern Queensland

down to Flinders Island in Bass Strait, so gardeners in the southern States can rest easy about its frost tolerance. While the species is normally white flowered, there is a beautiful pink-flowered cultivar called *Eleocarpus reticulatus* 'Prima Donna' that grows into a small tree about 10m high by several metres wide. The glossy dark green foliage has a lovely silvery leaf margin that softens its colour.

Eriostemon species and cultivars

The starry five-petalled flowers of this cheerful member of the citrus family (Rutaceae) are at their best from early to mid-spring. A recent name change has turned on its head the classification of this group, with many of the plants formerly known as *Eriostemon* being transferred to the genus *Philotheca*. (Refer to *Philotheca* for details of a number of plants that were formerly classified as *Eriostemon,* such as *Eriostemon myoporoides* and its cultivars.)

Eriostemon australasius (pink wax flower)
This is one of the species to remain an *Eriostemon*. It is perhaps the most spectacular member of the group but, as is often the case with plants of great beauty, it is rather difficult to cultivate. It normally bears beautiful, pink waxy flowers, 2–3cm in size, in profusion from early to mid-spring and the plant can grow to a height of 2m by 1m wide. The flowers are long lasting and are great to cut for indoor decoration. The pink wax flower does require very well-drained sandy soils to thrive and grows well in dappled shade through to full sun. It will tolerate light to moderate frosts and limited dry periods.

Eriostemon australasius 'Brilliance'
This is a rather stunning white-flowered selection made by Merricks Nursery in Victoria. It is a neat, small shrub growing to approximately 1m high by 1m wide, and features massed white, waxy flowers from August to November. 'Brilliance' makes an excellent flowering specimen for the garden bed or large container. Cultivation is the same as for *Eriostemon australasius*.

Eucalyptus species

No other continent is so dominated by one group of trees as is Australia by the eucalypts. In all but the driest of deserts, the familiar gnarled form of the gum tree forms the backbone to the landscape. The temptation is to dismiss eucalypts as being a bit on the dull side with their often wispy, willowy foliage, and perhaps not worthy of garden space that can be filled with more interesting plants. When one delves further into this amazing group, however, one is struck by both the subtle beauty of the many bark and foliage types and by the often spectacular flowers and the fruits that follow them.

Eucalypts have unfortunately attained something of a bad name in the garden as people unwittingly plant forest giants in

inner city courtyards, only to be horrified years later at the monster they have created. This is a tragedy as there is a whole host of smaller eucalypts that are virtually unknown to gardeners. As it is such a big group, the eucalypts are divided here into smaller groups according to those grown for their foliage, flowers or bark.

All eucalypts require full sun to do their best, and they are adaptable to most soil types, although this does vary between the different species. They will survive and grow slowly without fertiliser but a handful of native plant slow-release fertiliser in spring will see them rocket away.

Foliage eucalypts

A feature of eucalypts is the variation in foliage at different stages of growth. A number of species produce beautiful blue juvenile foliage that has found its way into floral arrangements all over the world. Juvenile foliage, as the name suggests, is displayed early in the life of the tree. Luckily for gardeners, though, most eucalypts can be 'rejuvenated' through hard pruning. Many eucalypts possess a gnarled, swollen structure called a lignotuber, which allows them to develop a dwarf, multi-trunked mallee habit. A seemingly infinite number of new buds is held in the lignotuber, meaning that the many eucalypt species can be successfully pruned and kept as shrubs in the garden albeit with a reasonable amount of work. An added bonus is that the leaves of all of the foliage eucalypts described below are fantastic for cut flower arrangements.

Eucalyptus cinerea (Argyle apple)
This spectacular, silvery blue tree grows to 20m in height has travelled to gardens all over the world, such is the attraction of its glorious foliage. It also produces a pleasant display of white flowers in summer. It is extremely hardy to frost and adapts well to

most soils. It does tend to struggle somewhat in more humid climates such as Brisbane and coastal parts of Sydney.

Eucalyptus crenulata (silver gum)
This interesting eucalypt is a fairly rare species that occurs in a few valleys near Melbourne. It is a relatively small tree, growing 10–15m tall, with a bushy crown and a nice display of white flowers in summer. However, it is the silvery foliage that makes it a wonderful choice as a background plant to highlight stronger colours in the garden. It is very frost tolerant and is quite happy in damp soils as well.

Eucalyptus gunnii (cider gum)
The cider gum has long been grown in Europe for its gorgeous bluish foliage and its great hardiness to frost, a legacy of the climate in its native Tasmania. It does eventually lose its juvenile foliage and grows into a medium-sized tree about 20m tall. The small white flowers are not particularly conspicuous when they appear in summer. A smaller version of this species is the Tasmanian alpine cider gum (*Eucalyptus archeri*), which is a close relative of the cider gum and also has beautiful greyish blue juvenile foliage.

Eucalyptus pulverulenta (silver-leaved mountain gum)
Curiously, many of the outstanding foliage eucalypts come from the mountainous areas of the east coast and Tasmania. Perhaps the outstanding species in this regard is the silver-leaved mountain gum with its leathery, powdery, rounded foliage. It survives in two isolated pockets in the Great Dividing Range near Bredbo and Lithgow in New South Wales. This frost-hardy tree generally grows to only several metres in height, but its habit of producing a strong lignotuber means that it can be pruned as hard as desired every year to form a brilliant powdery-blue shrub. This species does best in drier climates but can still be grown in the Sydney region and similar climates if you are prepared to put up with a little bit of leaf spot.

Flowering eucalypts
Undoubtedly the pinnacle of ornamental eucalypts is reached in Western Australia. The bright colours and bold, ornate buds and gumnuts set these plants apart from their eastern cousins. From the gardener's point of view, the most beautiful flowering eucalypts are mallees, which are well suited to suburban gardens in climates that have drier summers such as Melbourne, Adelaide, Canberra and, of course, Perth. For details of these, refer to the section 'Flowering eucalypts for low-humidity regions' on page 74. The bad news is that the western species do not thrive in the humid coastal areas of eastern Australia such as Brisbane and Sydney. Generally, the flowering eucalypts require well-drained soil and full sun, and most can withstand mild frosts.

Eucalyptus caesia (gungurru)
The gungurru is one of the most popular of the large-flowered eucalypts with its bright red, pendent flowers and silvery, bell-shaped gumnuts. A cultivar called *Eucalyptus caesia* 'Silver Princess' has the largest flowers of all. This species does especially well throughout most of Victoria.

Eucalyptus curtisii (Plunkett mallee)
For those in the more humid regions there are some fascinating small mallee eucalypts native to such climates that can be tamed in the garden. The Plunkett mallee occurs naturally in a small area near Brisbane, and is an ideal species for subtropical areas. It has masses of white blossoms in spring and a very fast growth rate. It grows to a height of less than 10m in most garden situations and withstands moderate frosts.

Grevillea 'Misty Pink'

Grevillea 'Pink Parfait'

Grevillea 'Honey Gem' (background), and *Anigozathos* 'Bush Ranger' and *Banksia* 'Giant Candles' (foreground)

Grevillea 'Sandra Gordon'

Grevillea 'Superb'

Flowering eucalypts for low-humidity regions

There is a wide range of spectacular flowering eucalypts from Western Australia that are best suited to the drier summers of southern and inland Australia and they include the following.

Eucalyptus ficifolia (syn. *Corymbia ficifolia*) (red-flowering gum)

It is impossible for most gardeners to resist wanting this tree once they have seen a good specimen in full flower. It has a very limited distribution in the wild, in southwestern Western Australia, which perhaps explains why it really only thrives in areas of low humidity. Sensational specimens can be found throughout southern Australia where it grows into a large tree and is covered in big clusters of blossoms in summer. The flower colour is highly variable in seed-raised specimens and can be anything from fire engine red to orange, pink or white. It is not a tree that performs well in Sydney and climates further north—the trees will survive and flower but they usually have a scrappy appearance. For subtropical gardeners, there is a new series of hybrids between *Eucalyptus ficifolia* and *E. ptychocarpa* (syn. *Corymbia ptychocarpa*), the swamp bloodwood from northern Australia. Going by the cultivar names 'Summer Pink' (pink flowered) and 'Summer Beauty' (red flowered), these new grafted plants have been out for several years and show great promise for lovers of red-flowering gum.

Eucalyptus luehmanniana (yellow-top mallee ash)

This delightful mallee is worth growing for the flower buds alone as they are ornate, silver in colour, and ideal for floral arrangements. Like most eucalypts, it is able to thrive in dry conditions and responds exceptionally well to pruning. If left to its own devices, it will grow to about 10m in height, but, for best ornamental value, it should be trimmed every year to make it more bushy.

Eucalyptus crucis (silver mallee)

This is a compact tree that grows to 15m in height with brilliant silver foliage and buds and yellow flowers.

Eucalyptus erythrocorys (Illyarrie)

This smallish tree grows to less than 10m in height. Its absolutely spectacular, large yellow flowers are preceded by a bud that has fire-engine red caps which are a feature in their own right.

Eucalyptus macrocarpa (mottlecah, rose of the west)

This is the largest flowered of all the eucalypts, with bright red flowers up to 10cm in size. It also has gorgeous blue foliage, which is a year-round feature of this mallee. It grows to no more than 5m in height, making it a perfect choice for smaller gardens.

Eucalyptus torquata (coral gum)

Another small tree growing to about 10m in height, this eucalypt has dark green, sickle-shaped leaves and produces fabulous displays of soft red flowers and intricately shaped coral-like buds that add to the interest of this hardy species. It is widely planted in Western Australia and makes an excellent street tree.

Eucalyptus woodwardii (lemon-flowered gum)

Although this is a sometimes straggly tree that grows to 15m in height, it is highlighted by the large, soft yellow flowers that are borne in profusion in spring. The foliage is typically gum leaf in shape and is a pleasing grey-green colour.

Beautifully barked eucalypts

The wonderful colours and textures of the bark of many eucalypts can add a lot of year-round interest to a garden design.

Eucalyptus citriodora (syn. *Corymbia citriodora*) (lemon-scented gum)
The lemon-scented gum has the obvious attraction of its beautifully perfumed leaves, which can be readily enjoyed after a shower of rain releases the essential oils. For the colour-conscious gardener, the sensuous powdery-white trunk is reason enough to plant this adaptable eucalypt. Its position in a garden needs to be carefully considered, however, as it can grow to 20–30m in height and is prone to shedding large branches. This makes it suitable for large gardens only and even then it should be planted well away from any buildings. It is well worth the trouble if you can fit it into your garden.

Eucalyptus maculata (syn. *Corymbia maculata*) (spotted gum)
Like its cousin the lemon-scented gum, this is also a large tree and is best suited to big gardens. Its great feature is its beautifully mottled bark that varies from pinks and creams to blue-grey tones at different times of the year. The beautiful trunk also displays itself very well.

Grevillea species and cultivars

One of the key groups of Australian plants in planning for year-round colour is the grevilleas. It is hard to know where to begin with this wonderfully diverse genus of plants as there are more than 300 wild species and dozens and dozens of fantastic cultivars specially selected for the garden.

Generally speaking, grevilleas grow and flower best in full sun, although there are also shade-tolerant types, such as the rare *Grevillea shiresii*, that flower well in sheltered positions. Grevilleas occur in virtually all habitats throughout Australia and it is important to choose one that is best suited to your garden's climate. The species range from the elegant *G. victoriae*, which comes from the high country of the Australian Alps, to the prostrate forms of the spectacular *G. banksii* which can be found growing on the coastal headlands of the region around Maryborough in Queensland.

Grevilleas also come in all shapes, sizes and flower colours, ranging from trees such as the silky oak (*Grevillea robusta*) to shrubs and groundcovering plants. Within a single species, there can be a range of growth habits and colours. The popular garden plant *G. banksii* comes in a number of forms, from prostrate small-flowered red, white or bicoloured forms to red or white forms that can grow as small trees, with various sized, dense shrub forms also possible.

Grevilleas are generally fairly trouble free in the garden, with very few pest problems. When and if they do get a problem, the plant will generally grow through it without the need for chemicals. Root rot may cause problems, however, particularly where drainage is not good. If plants show signs of water stress, even when well watered, then root rot is the usual cause and a soil drench of a systemic fungicide is worthwhile.

Low-phosphorus native plant fertilisers are highly recommended, particularly the slow-release types which can be applied at the beginning of spring for best results. A couple of light prunings through the warmer months will result in bushy compact plants. As Australians have come to accept and embrace the extraordinary diversity and beauty of our fauna and flora, gardeners are increasingly turning to groups such as the grevilleas which are superbly adapted to Australian soils and climatic extremes. Grevilleas offer the great bonus of being a magnet for birdlife, thus offering gardeners the possibility of creating a

The happy wanderer (*Hardenbergia*)

The stream lily (*Helmholtzia glaberimma*) is a wonderful shade plant

Hibbertia miniata is best grown in a pot to ensure correct drainage

habitat in their backyard, rather than a sterile collection of exotic species that often struggle with unfamiliar climatic extremes.

Grevilleas generally respond very well to pruning, although it should be mentioned that the foliage of a number of species can cause skin rashes so it is best to wear long sleeves and gloves when you are likely to be in close contact with the foliage.

One group of grevilleas has the fantastic quality of flowering all year round. The ever-blooming form of *Grevillea banksii* has been the parent of many interesting hybrid cultivars, some from deliberate breeding projects while others have arisen as chance seedlings from birds pollinating the flowers in garden situations. For those in warmer climates that do not experience heavy frosts, the 'Queensland' grevilleas (grevilleas with large brush-shaped flower heads like *G. banksii*) make for wonderful year-round

Isopogon cuneatus backed by *Dryandra formosa*

colour. This group has a flowering peak in winter, and it is a great sight at a time when lots of the exotic trees and shrubs look drab and uninteresting. In addition to the splashes of colour they produce, they are also irresistible to some of our more spectacular birds such as lorikeets and honeyeaters. Most of these plants have a silvery green fern-shaped leaf with the flowers in brush-shaped clusters prominently displayed on the ends of the stems. Generally speaking, this group of grevilleas requires an open, sunny position and good drainage to perform at their best and ideally should be given some protection from the wind as they can be uprooted during bad storms. Most of these grevilleas will also flower throughout the year but there is certainly a healthy peak in winter.

Fairly savage pruning (removing up to about one-third of the plant) is extremely important after a flush of flowers. Such pruning may necessitate removing some flower buds, but this sacrifice is well rewarded by the creation of a compact plant that can even be considered for use as a hedge.

Grevillea cultivars
There are many fabulous grevillia cultivars to choose from, with some of the best ones listed below.

Grevillea 'Bronze Rambler'
This is a vigorous groundcovering shrub that can spread up to 5m in width. The leaves are 15cm long by 4cm wide, and have many deep lobes. The leaves and stems are a lovely bronze colour, particularly when the growth is new, and this is a very attractive feature all year round. The toothbrush-shaped flower heads are 5cm long and are a rather subtle, dark pink. They are produced throughout the warmer months. This has proved to be a cultivar that is suitable for most climates and soil

types. It likes sun or semi-shade, tolerates poor drainage and frosts, and responds well to regular hard pruning. This cultivar is great for covering extensive embankments, and also makes a great weeping standard plant when grafted onto Grevillea robusta (silky oak). The bold foliage colour can be used to contrast with lighter-coloured plants in the larger landscape picture.

Grevillea 'Honey Gem'
This is a medium-sized to tall shrub (3–6m tall by 2–4m wide) with large, fern-like, dark green leaves that are attractive in their own right. Bright orange flower heads up to 15cm long are borne prolifically at the ends of the branches. Flowering tends to be mainly through winter and spring rather than all year round. It tends to grow more vigorously than most others of this group of grevilleas and so must be pruned hard at the end of its main flowering period in spring. This one has proved to be the best orange-flowered grevillea in the 'Queensland' grevillea category to date. The rich orange it brings to the garden is a unique hue.

Grevillea 'Ivanhoe'
This medium-sized shrub can grow up to 5m high by 5m wide. It has an attractive, long, lobed leaf, and pinkish red, toothbrush-shaped flower heads, up to several centimetres long, in profusion through the warmer months. This grevillea is very widely grown in the southern States of Australia and adapts well to most soil types provided the drainage is good. It flowers best in full sun but will grow in light shade as an understorey plant, and can cope with moderate frosts and drought conditions as well. Regular pruning, removing 20 to 30 per cent after flowering, will create a very bushy shrub that is ideal for screening and hedging. The pinkish new growth in spring is also a subtle colour feature.

Grevillea 'Misty Pink'

This is a bushy, medium-sized shrub (3–4m tall by 2–3m wide) with silvery grey, lobed leaves about 15cm long. The flower heads are 15cm long, and are produced continuously with peaks in autumn and winter. Individual flowers are a lovely pink with cream-coloured tips (styles). Its compact habit makes it very suitable for small gardens. Regular pruning is a must to develop a stunning garden plant. Flower heads are not as long as those on *Grevillea* 'Moonlight' (listed below) but there are plenty of them and their subtle colouring makes this plant a worthy choice for those wanting pink in their gardens.

Grevillea 'Moonlight'

Perhaps the best all-round performer of the 'Queensland' grevilleas, this is an upright shrub (3–4m high by 1.5m wide) with fine, large (15–20cm long), fern-like, olive green foliage. The creamy white flower heads, 20–25cm long, are borne in profusion all year round. Its clear, light colour distinguishes it from other grevilleas in this group. A favourite in this spectacular group of large-flowered grevilleas, it is rarely without a good display of flowers in frost-free areas and responds extremely well to pruning.

Grevillea 'Pink Parfait'

This cultivar is very similar to *Grevillea* 'Misty Pink' (listed above) in appearance and habit except that it has rosy pink flowers without the cream-coloured tips. It also flowers all year round and the flowers are a fantastic, darker shade of pink than the more subtle 'Misty Pink'.

Grevillea 'Poorinda Blondie'

This is a shrub that grows up to 4m high by 5–6m wide, with long, lobed leaves similar to those of *Grevillea* 'Ivanhoe' (listed opposite) which have a reddish tinge when young. It has yellow, toothbrush-shaped flower heads, several centimetres long, throughout spring and summer. It is very similar to 'Ivanhoe' in all respects except that the flower colour is an interesting yellow tone. It also makes an excellent screen or hedge, while the foliage adds an interesting textural element to the garden.

Grevillea 'Poorinda Peter'

This is a spreading shrub, growing to 4m high by 6m wide, that has deeply lobed leaves up to 15cm long. The foliage is a very striking, purple colour when young, before aging to dark green. The reddish purple, toothbrush-shaped flower heads are several centimetres long, and are conspicuous in the warmer months of the year. This is an incredibly hardy plant that will tolerate a wide range of soil types and climatic conditions throughout the southern States of Australia. Full sun to moderate shade is best, and it is also frost tolerant. Pruning up to 25 per cent of the branches on an annual basis will keep it compact, but even unpruned it retains a pleasing ascending shape. The coppery tones of the new growth are the best colour feature of 'Poorinda Peter', and it is perfect for screens and hedges and provides a pleasing backing foliage for floral arrangements.

Grevillea 'Poorinda Royal Mantle'

This groundcovering, vigorously spreading shrub (up to 8m in width) is the most commonly cultivated prostrate grevillea due to its outstanding adaptability to a wide range of climates and soil types (although it is not at home in the subtropical climates of coastal Queensland). The leaves are up to 15cm long, usually lobed, and are a very beautiful purplish colour when young. Masses of red, toothbrush-shaped flower heads are produced through the warmer months of the year, and these are a feature of the plant. It is a great plant for covering large

Black flowers can be introduced into your garden with the creeper *Kennedia nigricans*

The black kangaroo paw (*Macropidia fullginosa*)

The fruit of the spiny-headed mat rush (*Lomandra longifolia*)

areas in the garden that receive full sun or light shade and have reasonably well-drained soil. It responds well to pruning, whether it be heavy or light, and makes an outstanding weeping standard plant when grafted onto *Grevillea robusta* (silky oak) rootstock.

Grevillea 'Robyn Gordon'
This is a small to medium-sized shrub (2m tall by up to 3m wide) with bright green new leaves. The leaves are highly divided and have a somewhat ferny appearance and are about 20cm long. The bright red flowers, about 15cm long, are borne in spectacular clusters all year round. This is a very adaptable grevillea, well suited to subtropical and temperate climates and tolerating moderate frosts. It grows well in a range of soils, from sands to clays, and responds brilliantly to heavy pruning, which should preferably be done in spring. 'Robyn Gordon' is probably the best known Australian plant in cultivation and deservedly so. It has been a brilliant performer in general, however, a couple of points need to be watched. Firstly, like many other grevilleas, the foliage can cause skin rashes, and, secondly, it can be disfigured by the fungus sooty mould which causes black spotting of the stems and foliage. However, a good hard prune will cure most of its problems.

Grevillea 'Sandra Gordon'
This is a tall shrub to small tree (3–10m high by 2–3m wide) with silvery green, lobed leaves up to 25cm long. The clear yellow flower heads, up to 15cm long, are produced in clusters at the ends of branches throughout the autumn and winter months. This is the best bright yellow of the 'Queensland' grevilleas. It is an extremely vigorous grower and should be pruned back by 30 to 40 per cent at the end of its flowering period. The silvery foliage is a pleasing colour bonus all year round.

Grevillea 'Sunkissed Waters'
This is a variegated form of *Grevillea* 'Poorinda Royal Mantle' (listed on page 79) and so is identical in all aspects except that the foliage is light green with a thin band of creamy white on the margin. New growth is scarlet to scarlet-pink.

Grevillea 'Superb'
This plant has very similar parentage to *Grevillea* 'Robyn Gordon' (listed opposite) and is very similar in all characteristics except that it has bright pinkish orange flowers and tends to be a naturally denser, more vigorous plant as well. This cultivar should be used where you are looking for a brighter colour than the dark red flowers of 'Robyn Gordon'.

Grevillea species
As well as the grevillea cultivars already covered (most of which are hybrids between different species), there are many grevillea species that have a place in our gardens.

Grevillea alpina (mountain grevillea)
For those in cooler climates looking for colourful grevilleas, it is hard to go past the mountain grevillea with its many flower colour forms (white, cream, green, pink, red, yellow, orange and combinations). There are numerous selections of this species in cultivation, and they vary from groundcovers to shrubs up to 4m tall by about 2m wide. This species grows at a range of altitudes in the mountainous woodland country of southeastern Australia, giving it good frost tolerance and a preference for lightly shaded conditions. Hard pruning into old wood is not recommended; rather, give the plant a light trim after flowering.

Grevillea banksii (dwarf silky oak, Banks's grevillea)
This rather amazing grevillea can vary from a groundcover (such as the cultivar 'Ruby

Red') to a small tree that is 7–8m tall by 3m wide. It has attractive, dark green, lobed leaves, and spectacular brush-shaped flower heads, up to 20cm long, in red or white. The most commonly available form in cultivation is *Grevillea banksii* 'Forsters', a cultivar that is distinguished by its ever-blooming, compact habit. It grows to about 3m in height, and has adapted well to cultivation throughout the warmer climates of southern Australia where it performs best in well-drained soils in full sun or part shade. It is, however, somewhat frost sensitive.

Grevillea barklyana (large-leaf grevillea)
This species is a large shrub, growing up to 10m high by 5–6m wide, and it has attractively lobed, silvery, mid-green foliage. The pale pink, toothbrush-shaped flower heads are up to 10cm long, and appear throughout the year with a peak in the warmer months. A quick-growing grevillea suitable for screening and hedging, it is frost tolerant, withstands poor drainage, and is best grown in part shade.

Grevillea hilliana (white yiel yiel)
This is a small, spreading tree, growing to about 15m high by 10m wide, with beautiful, glossy green foliage that has a silky white underside. It produces rather spectacular ivory-coloured, brush-shaped flower heads, up to 20cm long, from late winter to early summer. It tolerates light frosts, prefers deep well-drained soils, and is best left to develop its own shape without pruning.

Grevillea juniperina (juniper grevillea)
This rather prickly shrub has prostrate forms but it can also grow to 4m tall by up to 5m wide. It has dark green, needle-like leaves that are densely packed on the stems and are interspersed with spidery flower heads that may be cream, yellow, apricot,

orange or red and are prominently displayed. It is a very adaptable species that thrives in semi-arid to subtropical climates, and it adapts to most soil types including those with less than perfect drainage. This species responds well to pruning and can be used as either a groundcover (prostrate forms) or as a screen or hedge plant.

Grevillea lanigera (woolly grevillea)
Another species for cool and warm climates alike is the woolly grevillea which has many different forms in the wild, from prostrate plants to shrubs up to 2–3m tall, with the spidery flowers varying in colour from reddish pink to cream to lime green and cream. It adapts well to most Australian climatic zones and soil types, although it does prefer good drainage. It flowers from autumn through into summer and makes a good informal hedge or screen plant.

Grevillea robusta (silky oak)
This versatile tree grevillea has become popular in various parts of the world due to its spectacular flowering and relatively manageable size. It generally grows into a small tree about 10–15m in height, although it can grow much taller in ideal conditions. It adapts well to a range of soil and climatic conditions and will tolerate some frost. The golden orange flowers appear in profusion in spring, and the shiny, mid-green, lobed foliage is also an attractive feature.

Grevillea rosmarinifolia (rosemary grevillea)
The rosemary grevillea has been popular in cooler climates for decades due to its adaptability as a screen or hedge plant. Although there are prostrate forms, the commonly cultivated form grows to about 2–3m tall and wide. The dark green, needle-like foliage contrasts well with the red or pink flowers. This is a very tough plant that adapts to most soils and will survive hard

Robin red breast (*Melaleuca latenta*)

Grey-leafed honey myrtle (*Melaleuca incana*)

Melaleuca bracteata 'Revolution Gold'

Snow-in-summer (*Melaleuca linariifolia*)

Daisy bush (*Olearia phlogopappa*)

frosts. It requires very little maintenance apart from a light pruning after the main flowering period in winter to early summer.

Grevillea shiresii (blue grevillea)
This medium-sized shrub (3–6m tall by 2–5m wide) has rather subtle, greenish blue flowers that are very attractive to birds. The flowers are not prominently displayed as they are interspersed among the foliage. This grevillea is rather unusual in that it grows well in shady conditions and adapts well to moist soils. It tolerates light frosts and, from a colour point of view, the glossy, dark green foliage is its outstanding feature.

Grevillea victoriae (royal grevillea)
This dwarf to medium-sized shrub comes from the mountainous areas of southern New South Wales and eastern Victoria. It is a rather variable species, but the most common form in cultivation has red pendent flowers held prominently within the attractive, greyish green foliage. It prefers light shade and will tolerate the heaviest of frosts as well as a range of soil types. A light prune after the spring flowering period will develop a very nice screening plant.

Grafted grevilleas
There are a number of very beautiful and unusual grevillea species that come from the drier climates of Australia. Traditionally, these species have been very difficult to grow in the more humid climates of eastern Australia, however, great progress has been made in the last decade or so by grafting them onto hardy rootstocks such as the silky oak (*Grevillea robusta*) and G. 'Poorinda Royal Mantle'. Some of the more spectacular and successful species to look for include G. *bipinnatifida*, G. *candelabroides*, G. *dielsiana*, G. *dryandroides*, G. *formosa*, G. *petrophiloides* and G. *thyrsoides*. Specialist Australian plant nurseries would be the best place to seek a range of grafted grevilleas.

Hakea species and cultivars
Hakea is a large genus, with about 150 species, in the same family as the banksias and grevilleas (Proteaceae). There are a number of showy members of the genus that are well worth considering for the garden. Most hakeas are small to medium-sized shrubs and generally speaking, they should be grown in full sun and well-drained soil conditions. Give them a light prune after flowering and a handful of low-phosphorus native plant fertiliser and you will be well rewarded.

Hakea bucculenta (red pokers)
This very spectacular Western Australian hakea grows to a height of about 5m and has masses of bright orange-red flowers along the upper branches from late winter to early summer. For best results, it should be grown in a climate with a dry summer; however, it has also been successful in other climates when grown as a grafted plant on rootstock such as *Hakea salicifolia* from eastern Australia. It does require excellent drainage but will withstand moderate frosts. Red pokers is a very beautiful hakea that is well worth a bit of extra effort in the garden.

Hakea laurina (pincushion hakea)
This rather showy hakea has long been successful in cultivation, with its red and cream, globe-shaped flower heads, up to 7cm in diameter, being a feature through autumn and winter. It is a medium-sized shrub usually reaching at least 5m in height, and it makes an ideal screen plant. The foliage is a pleasing mid-green colour and is rather dense. It has proved to be fairly adaptable over a range of climates.

Hakea trinuera
Indigenous to the north coast of New South Wales, this little-known hakea is well suited to subtropical areas where many other hakeas will not grow well. It forms a

medium-sized dense shrub to about 5m tall, with rather pleasing, glossy green leaves that are interspersed with the fragrant red flowers massed along the outer branches. The species may be hard to find in nurseries but is worth the effort as it is a spectacular plant, particularly for gardeners around Sydney and Brisbane.

Hardenbergia species and cultivars

The native sarsparilla (*Hardenbergia violacea*) is found in every State of Australia with the exception of Western Australia and as you would expect it is extremely adaptable. In the wild, it is usually a scrambler or a climber (if there is support available); however, there are also wild forms that have an upright habit so you can have your cake and eat it too by growing a compact, shrubby cultivar known as 'Mini-haha' (listed below). Hardenbergias are very adaptable as far as soil goes. They grow in full sun or light shade and will tolerate some frost. An annual pruning after flowering is perhaps the only maintenance required.

Hardenbergia violacea 'Free 'n' Easy'
This climbing or trailing form makes an excellent groundcover growing to about 1m or more in diameter or it can be trained onto a support. It has large, lance-shaped leaves (up to 125mm long by up to 50mm wide) with reddish bronze new growth. It produces white flowers with a hint of pink in profusion in spring. As with all forms of this variable species, the display of flowers is very showy.

Hardenbergia violacea 'Mini-haha'
This is a delightful, small, upright, bushy shrub that grows to 15–30cm tall by 30–50cm wide. This form has smallish, bright green leaves with reddish bronze new growth. It bears dark mauve flowers in profusion in spring.

Hardenbergia violacea 'Pink Fizz'
Unlike 'Mini-haha' (listed previously), this is a climbing or trailing small shrub that makes an excellent groundcover, spreading to 1m or more in diameter, or it can be trained onto a support. It has medium-sized, lance-shaped, dark green leaves with reddish bronze new growth, and dark pink flowers in profusion in spring. This plant is a very good option for bringing a bold splash of pink into your spring garden.

Helmholtzia glaberimma (stream lily)

This is a wonderful plant from the more subtropical areas of Australia, although it will grow well in a protected spot in southern Australia. The stream lily grows wild in dense shade on the floor of the rainforest in northeastern New South Wales, and the dark green, strap-like leaves form a clump about 1m in height and width when fully grown. The foliage is reason alone to grow this rather interesting, clumping plant, but it is complemented by the dramatic pink flower sprays in late spring. This is a plant of enormous value to gardeners because it is one that will flower reliably in dense shade—it might even be considered an Australian rival for the clivea. The plant is somewhat lily-like in appearance, requires plenty of moisture, and will tolerate light frosts.

Hibbertia species (guinea flowers)

These shrubs and climbers are noted for their clear, bright yellow flowers. The most common species in cultivation are twiners that can climb if given support. They are reasonably adaptable plants and, with more than 150 species to choose from in Australia, there is a hibbertia for almost any habitat. Local native plant nurseries are worth checking to see if they have any local species.

Pandorea jasminoides 'Southern Belle' backed by snow-in-summer (*Melaleuca linariifolia*)

Pine-leafed geebung (*Persoonia pinifolia*)

Pimelea ferniginea 'Magenta Mist'

Hibbertia dentata (trailing guinea flower)
The gorgeous bronze-green foliage of this plant is a year-round feature and is highlighted by large, bright yellow flowers that appear in profusion all through spring and sporadically at other times of the year. It is a twining plant by nature and will climb if given support, otherwise it makes a lovely groundcover that creates a bronze-toned carpet in your garden. It can spread up to 1m in diameter, and thrives best in partly shaded positions. It likes a soil with moderate drainage and is rather frost tender.

Hibbertia scandens (snake vine)
The snake vine is an incredibly hardy plant that is capable of growing in frontline coastal conditions as it commonly grows on foredunes at various beaches along the New South Wales and Queensland coastlines. It flowers sporadically all year round and provides a welcome display of sunny yellow flowers throughout winter. The common name comes from its chunky, robust stems that are capable of either climbing a support or sprawling along the ground and creating a dense cover in a wide variety of soils and climates. The large, silky leaves have a silvery appearance when new and provide a green carpet when this plant is used as a groundcover. In the garden, it prefers well-drained soils and will grow equally well in full sun or part shade.

Hibiscus species
Australia has a number of rather spectacular species from this showy member of the cotton family (Malvaceae). The Australian species are generally small to large shrubs found in warmer climates such as those of northern Australia.

Hibiscus heterophyllus (native rosella)
Looking much like an exotic hibiscus, the native rosella grows to about 5m in height. The spectacular flowers are up to 15cm in size and come in a range of colours, including pink, yellow and white with a red centre. The large, dark green, finger-like leaves are up to 20cm long. It is a fast-growing plant that needs a well-drained soil and is surprisingly frost tolerant. An added bonus is that it flowers throughout the warmer months of the year.

Hymenosporum flavum (native frangipani)
If you are looking to add deep yellow, fragrant, trumpet-like flowers and dark green foliage to your garden, then this tree is for you. Native frangipani has a flower not unlike the exotic frangipani (to which it is totally unrelated) with a rather similar perfume. It is usually a smallish tree under garden conditions (about 10m tall) and has a very interesting pyramid shape to it. The cream-coloured flowers are 2–4cm in size, age to a deep yellow, and are produced in mid-spring. The tree tends to retain its lower branches and so it is well worth planting it beside a path or, better still, beside a balcony so that it can set the stage for romantic interludes on those warm spring nights! This plant is rather frost tender and is best for gardens in warmer climates such those of Sydney and Brisbane.

Hypocalymma species
This is a lovely group of the myrtle family (Myrtaceae) that is increasing in popularity due to its adaptability and lovely displays of flowers. There are a couple of species in particular that can be recommended.

Hypocalymma angustifolium (white myrtle)
This is a very attractive, small shrub growing to 1–2m in height and width. It has adapted very well to the southern States of Australia and produces a showy display of fluffy white or white and pink flowers throughout spring. It has soft, needle-like leaves that have a pleasant aroma when crushed. It

prefers a well-drained soil and light shade, and can be pruned to whatever shape you desire after flowering has finished.

Hypocalymma robustum (Swan River myrtle)
This delightful plant grows naturally over a wide area of southwestern Western Australia and has proved to be adaptable in cultivation, particularly in drier climates. The fluffy pink flowers are borne on a small upright shrub and have a wonderful sweet yet subtle perfume. It makes a superb cut flower—the fragrance can be detected across a room. The yellow pollen-bearing anthers make a pleasing contrast with the pink petals and give the flowers an extra charm. The main requirement for growing the Swan River myrtle is a well-drained soil, preferably on the sandy side. It prefers light shade, responds well to pruning after flowering, and can tolerate light frosts

Indigofera australis (indigo bush, Australian indigo)

The indigo bush is a very appropriate name for this versatile shrub from the pea family (Fabaceae). This plant is a smallish shrub, growing to about 2–3m in height and width, and has beautiful, ferny, dark green foliage. From late winter to spring, it lights up with pink or purple flowers. It is very adaptable to different soil types, prefers a shady position in the garden, and responds well to light pruning after flowering.

Isopogon species (drumsticks)

The drumsticks are an interesting group within the protea family (Proteaceae). Their common name is derived from the conical shape of the seed pods that are retained indefinitely on the plant. Isopogons generally grow best in sandy, well-drained soil and full sun or very light shade. Established plants will benefit from a light pruning after flowering as well as a small dose of a low-phosphorus native plant fertiliser.

Isopogon anemonifolius (broad-leaf drumsticks)
The intricately designed, yellow flower heads (about 4cm in diameter) of this small shrub (growing to 2m tall and wide) are a prominent feature of the plant in spring. The light green leaves have anemone-like lobes and are also an attractive feature. A couple of dwarf forms that grow to about 30cm in height have recently been introduced to the nursery trade and are worth looking for. This is a relatively hardy species from New South Wales coastal areas but it will not tolerate heavy frosts.

Isopogon cuneatus
This small shrub grows to about 2m tall and wide, and features stunning purplish pink flower heads that are about 5cm in diameter. It is a Western Australian species that requires dry summers and frost-free conditions to really thrive. This counts out the more humid climates of much of the east coast of Australia; however, it is quite well suited to large areas of southern and inland Australia. It is worth persisting with this plant if you like its exotic colour.

Isotoma species

This little-known group of Australian plants belongs to the lobelia family (Lobeliaceae) and, like that family, *Isotoma* species have predominantly blue flowers, although there are also species with white flowers. As a group they are great for rockeries, mass displays and for container culture. They require lots of sun and reasonably good drainage. Most species are perennial and will regenerate quite well if pruned after flowering. One thing to watch with these plants is that they produce a milky sap that can irritate the skin. This is only likely when you are pruning or weeding the plants and a little care will keep you safe.

Isotoma axillaris (Australian harebell)
This is by far the most popular species in cultivation and can be used to create a lovely mass display. It grows to no more than 30cm in height and can spread to 1m in diameter. The starry flowers are relatively large, up to 4cm in size, and vary from pale to dark blue. The plants have a useful life of 2–3 years but can be easily regenerated by taking cuttings in late summer.

Isotoma fluviatilis
This little-known perennial makes a lovely soft, emerald green carpet that is a mass of tiny (1cm in size) starry, pale to dark blue flowers from spring through into autumn, making it an exceptional choice for pot culture and courtyard gardens where its miniature habit can be enjoyed at close quarters. It is hardy to frosts and requires constant moisture to thrive. It is one of those wonderful 'magic pudding' type plants that you can take little pieces off for propagation and they are replaced by the plant in no time.

Jasminum suavissimum (native jasmine)

Jasmine is not a plant we normally associate with natives but Australia has about a dozen species, mainly distributed in subtropical areas of northern Australia. *Jasminum suavissimum* is probably the most popular Australian species in cultivation, producing the familiar white, perfumed, tubular flowers associated with the name 'jasmine'. This species is a twining plant that is far less invasive than the traditional exotic jasmines. It can be used either as a groundcover or as a climbing plant. It tolerates light frosts and is covered in flowers from spring through to summer. In the garden, it prefers full sun, responds well to hard pruning, and is drought tolerant.

The sweetly scented flowers of native daphne (*Pittosporum undulatum*)

Native mint bush (*Prostanthra* 'Poorinda Balleria')

Oval-leafed mint bush (*Prostanthera ovalifloia*)

Kennedia species

This is a very useful group of climbing pea-flowered plants that generally have rather spectacular red flowers and interesting foliage. They grow in many and varied habitats and are very adaptable to garden conditions. They make excellent groundcovers for embankments or can be used as climbers if given a support to help them off the ground. They are generally very hardy to frost and will happily adapt to almost any soil type. They will also grow on the sniff of an empty fertiliser bag.

Kennedia nigricans (black coral pea)
This extraordinary plant is a rarity in the world flora—a black-flowered climber. It is an extremely vigorous climber and is perhaps unsuitable for small gardens unless you are prepared to constantly prune it back to a manageable-sized plant. However, it is hard to resist the fascinating, bicoloured black and yellow-green flowers that are borne throughout spring. As a bonus, it attracts nectar-feeding birds to its spectacular flowers.

Kennedia prostrata (running postman)
As its common name suggests, running postman is normally a prostrate plant but it can also be encouraged to climb. This adaptable species is found in every State of Australia and is as tough as nails. It has mid-green foliage that has a pleasing wavy margin. The bright red flowers have a vibrant yellow blotch at their centre and appear throughout early spring and summer. A light pruning after the flowering period will keep the plant looking its best.

Kennedia rubicunda (dusky coral pea)
This is another very widespread species that is found throughout the eastern States. It has deep red flowers in spring, and these are complemented by restful, dark green foliage. The species grows in a range of

habitats, including coastal sand dunes, and this gives a clue as to how adaptable it is to all sorts of garden conditions. This is a good foundation plant when establishing a garden, as are all the kennedias.

Kunzea species

This attractive member of the myrtle family (Myrtaceae) is closely related to the callistemons and melaleucas and is distinguished by the flower heads being prominently displayed at the ends of the stems. It is a rather interesting group of plants for the garden.

Kunzea ambigua (tick bush)
A medium-sized shrub that can grow several metres in height and width, the tick bush becomes covered in masses of perfumed white flowers in mid-spring. It has fairly fine foliage that forms a dense cover over the plant, making this a good hedge or screen plant. This species does well in coastal conditions, tolerates light frosts, and should be given as much sun as possible for best flowering.

Kunzea baxteri (crimson kunzea)
This is a lovely weeping shrub growing to 3m in height and width. It has rather spectacular red bottlebrushes from autumn through to spring. The flowers are tipped with yellow pollen-bearing anthers. It requires a sunny, frost-free spot with well-drained soil, and responds well to pruning back to behind the spent flowers.

Lagunaria patersonii (Norfolk Island hibiscus)

This small tree grows to about 10m tall and is one of the best plants for areas with coastal exposure. It has medium-sized, glossy, dark green foliage interspersed in summer with masses of pink flowers that are like miniature hibiscus flowers (not surprising as they are in the same family).

The plant adapts well to most soil types provided the drainage is reasonable and it will also grow well in inland areas in all but the frostiest of climates. It does not require pruning and is drought hardy. It has a long flowering period from summer through to autumn. Beware of the seed pods, which contain hairs that can be irritating to the eyes and skin.

Lechenaultia species

This spectacular group of Western Australian plants is one of the brightest and most colourful of all Australian plants. There are a couple of dozen species that vary in flower colour from royal blue to pillar box red, yellow and virtually all shades in between. Unfortunately, however, lechenaultias have proved to be very difficult in cultivation, particularly in areas with high humidity, and for this reason alone are not widely available. So here we describe only the hardiest species, *Lechenaultia biloba*.

Lechenaultia biloba (blue lechenaultia)
This dwarf shrub usually grows to about 50cm or less in height, with beautiful blue flowers from winter through into summer. It has lovely fine, grey-green foliage and benefits from tip-pruning in the early stages of development as well as a light trim after flowering. It is not frost tolerant and requires full sun and very well-drained soil. The best way to grow this and other lechenaultias is in a good quality potting mix in a pot or hanging basket. Even if they only provide one flowering in your garden, it will be unforgettable.

Leptospermum species and cultivars (tea trees)

Some exciting new tea trees have become available in the last few years, and many more are to come. Breeders have been working with the very large-flowered species, such as *Leptospermum macrocarpum*, to create an entirely new range of spectacular cultivars to add to the selection of old-favourite tea trees already available.

The tea trees generally flower from early to mid-spring to summer, and are excellent plants for gardens that have soils with less than perfect drainage. Many wild species of tea tree can be found growing along the margins of creeks and rivers where the soil is often quite moist if not waterlogged.

Leptospermum 'Aphrodite'
This is small to medium-sized shrub, growing about 2m tall and wide, with a very dense branching habit. It has short, narrow, elliptical leaves that are interspersed with large (2cm in size), fiery pink flowers in late spring. This plant is one of a series of new cultivars bred by Peter Ollerenshaw of Bywong Nursery in the New South Wales Southern Tablelands. The fact that this and his other cultivars have been trialled in a cold climate suggests they will be very frost tolerant. The compact nature also means they need minimal pruning.

Leptospermum 'Pacific Beauty'
This is a vigorous groundcover growing to 30cm high by at least 1m wide. It has gorgeous, fine, lacy foliage and masses of pink buds that open white and are produced in profusion throughout spring. It is frost resistant and, while it responds well to pruning, it is such a compact plant that it rarely needs it. This cultivar is ideal for smaller gardens and for containers.

Leptospermum petersonii (lemon-scented tea tree)
This is a very reliable shrub that reaches 4–5m in height and a width of up to 3m. It produces an attractive display of numerous, small white flowers in early summer and has dense, light green foliage that has the most wonderful lemon perfume, which is

Scaevola 'Super Clusters'

Syzygium jambos, one of the fabulous lillypilly group

released when the leaves are brushed against or after a shower of rain. It is moderately frost hardy, and responds very well to pruning. It makes an excellent background or screen plant especially for gardens with a white colour theme.

Leptospermum polygalifolium 'Cardwell'
This compact shrub grows to about 2–3m tall by 2m wide and has a delightfully graceful weeping habit. The dense, deep green leaves are small and lance-shaped with the new growth having a pleasant reddish tinge. This is one of the most spectacular white-flowering shrubs in the Australian flora, with its wonderful display from late spring into summer. It makes an excellent feature or screen plant and can be relied upon for a dazzling display even under drought conditions. It should be given a light to moderate pruning immediately after flowering, depending on how compact you like your shrubs.

Leptospermum 'Rhiannon'
This is a small to medium-sized shrub growing about 2m tall and wide. The branches tend to grow horizontally, giving the plant an interesting shape, and are clothed in mid-green smallish leaves. In spring, it is covered with large (2cm in size), green-centred pink flowers amid the green foliage. It is another outstanding frost-tolerant release from Bywong Nursery and perhaps its only drawback is a relatively short flowering period.

New South Wales waratah (*Telopea speciosissima*)

Leptospermum rotundifolium 'Lavender Queen'

This is a dense, low-growing shrub reaching to about 1.5m tall by 1–2m wide. The deep green, small, rounded leaves have a pleasant perfume when brushed against. The stunning feature of this plant is the profusion of large (up to 3cm wide), pinkish purple flowers from mid- to late spring. The very large, glossy seed capsules persist on the branches and are quite ornamental in their own right. This plant makes a wonderful cut flower, a fact that enables you to prune the plant as well as enjoying it indoors. *Leptospermum rotundifolium* 'Julie Ann' is a cultivar that has similar characteristics to 'Lavender Queen' except that it is a prostrate shrub that generally grows no taller than 30cm. Both these cultivars are resistant to frost, and will respond well to pruning.

Lomandra species (mat rushes)

A group of plants that fits well into any style of garden is the mat rushes. These plants form large clumps in similar style to agapanthus and the plants have long strap-like leaves that can blend in with other clumping plants. They are primarily grown for the effect produced by their lovely mid-green foliage. A number of species of *Lomandra* are available from specialist Australian plant nurseries and are worthy of consideration if you are looking for clumping, green foliage plants.

Lomandra longifolia (spiny-headed mat rush)

This is the most popular species in cultivation and forms a clump up to 1m wide with shiny leaves about 70cm–1m long. In spring, the plants send up an interesting-looking flower stem that is yellow with a number of not too ferocious spines. The flower also has a distinctly sweet perfume that adds to its charm. It is incredibly adaptable to different soils and climates and is one of the hardier plants in the Australian flora. It will grow well in sun or light to moderate shade and is also frost resistant.

Macropidia fuliginosa (black kangaroo paw)

This plant is something of a Holy Grail for native plant enthusiasts with its lime green flowers being covered in jet-black hairs. The plant itself forms a small clump of about 50cm wide. Flowers are generally produced throughout spring, and the plant has a tendency to become semi-dormant through the heat of summer when it can be difficult to keep it free of root disease in humid climates such as Sydney and Brisbane. It is certainly better suited to climates with dry summers such as in southern Australia. The flower stems reach a height of 1.5m and the grey-green leaves are about 70cm long. The rather intricate, tubular flower folds back on itself to give it a rather exotic orchid-like appearance. Perhaps the best results are achieved by growing the plant in a large container (for example, 25cm in diameter) in full sun. Black kangaroo paw is mildly frost hardy and advice on maintenance is the same as for the other kangaroo paws (refer to *Anigozanthos*, pages 29–33).

Melaleuca species and cultivars

Apart from a range of colourful flowers and foliage, the melaleucas are also very valuable plants because of their ability to grow in poorly drained and even waterlogged soils. This makes them suitable for almost any garden as they will also thrive in well-drained soils provided they are given plenty of moisture and/or mulch. It is then simply a matter of choosing a species that is suited to your climate. It must be said that they will flower best in full sun. It is also worth mentioning that most melaleucas have a very vigorous root system that can cause problems with house foundations and pipes.

Melaleuca bracteata 'Revolution Gold'
'Revolution Gold' is a compact cultivar of this hardy species and it will grow to about 2m in height by up to 4m wide. It has rather beautiful golden yellow foliage for which it is named. It makes an excellent screen or background plant that will give a colourful lift to a dull corner of the garden. It is frost hardy and requires minimal maintenance. This cultivar also adapts very well to tropical and subtropical climates.

Melaleuca diosmifolia
Unusual, green bottlebrush flowers and densely packed, small, decorative leaves are the features of this species from the coastline of Western Australia. It grows to a height of 3m and spreads up to 2m wide. The dark green, formal foliage makes this an interesting choice as a hedge or screen plant. It is not frost hardy, but it can be pruned to whatever shape you desire.

Melaleuca hypericifolia (honey myrtle)
This rounded shrub can grow to 5m tall by several metres wide. The mid-green leaves (about 4cm in length) are attractive, and are interspersed with rusty red bottlebrushes that are about 5cm long and are rather showy in late spring and summer. It tolerates mild frosts and most soil types. There is a useful prostrate cultivar of this species known as *Melaleuca hypericifolia* 'Ulladulla Beacon' that is excellent for embankments and rockeries.

Melaleuca incana (grey-leafed honey myrtle)
The soft, grey-green foliage is the most ornamental feature of this attractive shrub that grows to 2–3m high by 2m wide. The smallish (3cm long), creamy yellow bottlebrushes are produced in late spring and early summer. It is reasonably frost hardy and can be clipped into a formal hedge. There is also a wonderful dwarf cultivar of this species known as *Melaleuca*

incana 'Velvet Cushion' that grows to about 1m in height and forms a tight bun-shaped shrub without the need for pruning. The grey-leafed honey myrtle is an outstanding plant for grey and silver garden themes, especially for hedging and screening.

Melaleuca laterita (robin red breast)
Large, orange-red, bottlebrush-like flowers (5cm long) in late spring and summer are the feature of this upright shrub that grows to 2m tall by 1m wide. The light green, linear leaves are about 1.5cm long and are a pleasant complement to the flowers. Unlike many melaleucas, this species does not tolerate poorly drained soils or heavy frost. However, under the right growing conditions, it will produce a spectacular floral display.

Melaleuca linariifolia (snow-in-summer)
This is a very hardy and versatile small tree that grows to about 10m in height by several metres wide. It has attractive, light-coloured papery bark that is complemented by a spectacular display of lacy white flowers in summer, as the common name would suggest. The species is particularly good in poorly drained or waterlogged conditions but is somewhat frost tender, particularly when young. There is also a wonderful dwarf form of this species known as 'Snowstorm' that has the same profuse flowering habit but only grows to 1.5m tall by 1.5m wide.

Melaleuca nesophila (western tea myrtle, pink melaleuca)
This dense, bushy shrub grows to about 4m in height by about 2m wide. The 2.5cm-long, oval-shaped leaves are a lovely bright green and are a feature in their own right when the plants are not in flower. The deep mauve flower heads are prominently displayed at the ends of the branches in summer. The species is frost hardy and

Fringe lily (*Thysanotus multiflorus*)

Australian bluebell (*Wahlenbergia gloriosa*)

tolerates poorly drained soils. There is also a compact cultivar of this species called 'Little Nessy', which has all the features of the species but only grows to a height of about 2m.

Melaleuca thymifolia (thyme honey myrtle) This is a very versatile and popular melaleuca that has given rise to several beautiful cultivars. The standard form of the species is a small shrub that grows to about 1m in height and width. It has small, light green leaves and dainty violet flowers in summer. It is very tolerant of poor drainage, is frost resistant, and benefits from a light prune in summer after flowering. This species has several very interesting and worthwhile cultivars, namely 'White Lace',

Scarlet feather flower (*Verticordia grandis*)

'Pink Lace' (light pink flowers) and 'Cotton Candy' (dark pink flowers). All three are very compact (similar to the parent species), and flower sporadically all year round with a definite peak in late spring and summer. Due to its compact habit, this is perhaps the most useful of all the melaleucas.

Melia azedarach (white cedar)

The white cedar is one of the few Australian natives that is deciduous, which makes it a very useful medium-sized tree that will attain a height of 10–15m by up to 10m in width. Because it loses its leaves in winter, it is ideal for situations where you want shade in summer but full sun in winter—such as for north-facing aspects. A further bonus with the white cedar is that the soft purple flowers have a very strong fragrance that is noticeable metres away from the tree. The only thing to watch with this plant is that it is often attacked by its very own moth, the white cedar moth (*Leptocneria reducta*). The caterpillars of this moth can be found at the base of the tree by day, and by night they become marauding fiends that can completely strip the tree of foliage if unchecked. Fortunately, the solution is simple—a hessian sack tied around the base of the tree provides a place where the caterpillars will gather. In the morning, the sack and caterpillars can be taken to a convenient slab of concrete where the caterpillars can be shaken out and jumped on—a much more satisfying control method than spraying chemicals!

Micromyrtus ciliata (fringed myrtle)

This compact member of the myrtle family (Myrtaceae) is generally less than 1m in height by about 1m in width, although there are some interesting prostrate forms available as well. Its small, dark green leaves give it a somewhat conifer-like appearance when it is not in flower. It produces masses of tiny white flowers that age to red throughout spring and summer, and it can be used as a cut flower, which will prune the plant at the same time. It needs a well-drained sunny position and is reasonably frost resistant.

Myoporum species (boobiallas)

The wonderfully named boobiallas are highly underrated as garden plants.

Myoporum floribundum (snow-in-summer)
This plant is unrelated to the melaleuca with which it shares a common name (*Melaleuca linariifolia*), but it is similarly spectacular in its own way. It is a spreading shrub growing to 3m in height and width. The linear leaves are long (up to 10cm) and weep gracefully from the horizontal branches. Tiny white flowers are borne profusely along the branches during spring and summer and are reminiscent of a light dusting of snow, hence the common name. It is frost resistant, needs well-drained soil, and prefers full sun but will perform satisfactorily in light shade.

Myoporum parvifolium (creeping boobialla)
This prostrate shrub can, under ideal conditions, spread up to 5m in width, but more commonly it reaches 1m or so. The rich green, linear leaves can sometimes take on an interesting purple hue. The tiny, star-like flowers come in either white or pink and are dotted through the foliage from spring through to summer. This species adapts well to a wide range of soil conditions and will tolerate moderate frosts; however, it is not well suited to subtropical or tropical climates.

Olearia species (daisy bushes)

This rather wonderful group of native daisies generally takes a shrubby form. Australia has about 130 species of these easy-to-grow plants and they generally provide a mass display of tiny daisies.

Olearia phlogopappa (dusty daisy bush)
This is perhaps the most widely grown olearia in cultivation and grows to about 2.5m tall and wide. The small, greyish to dark green leaves become smothered in little daisies through spring and summer. The species comes in a wide variety of flower colours such as white, pink, mauve and blue, all with a yellow centre. It will tolerate light frosts and is best grown in semi-shade. The plant should be pruned back several centimetres behind the flowers after they have finished. In addition to providing a colourful feature in the garden, the flowers also attract butterflies and can be cut for indoor decorations.

Ozothamnus species

This group is perhaps best described as shrubby everlasting daisies, with most of the 50 or so species producing flat-topped heads of masses of tiny flowers with papery bracts. They have long been included in the genus *Helichrysum*. While only one species is listed here—*Ozothamnus diosmifolius*—because of its ready availability, there are other species available from specialist native nurseries including the spectacular yellow-flowered species *O. obcordatus*.

Ozothamnus diosmifolius (rice flower, sago flower)
A medium-sized shrub growing to a height and width of 2m, this species has short, linear, dark green leaves that have a curious

curry-like fragrance when crushed. The individual pink or white everlasting flowers are massed together into attractive dome-shaped flower heads and are particularly useful as cut flowers. It is a quick-growing but sometimes short-lived plant that will perform best in full sun and it tolerates light frosts. It should be pruned both during and after flowering to prolong its useful life in the garden.

Pandorea species and cultivars
These glossy leaved, fast-growing climbers provide a wonderful splash of colour in the warmer months of the year.

Pandorea jasminoides (bower of beauty)
This vigorous climber will expand to cover whatever support it is given. It has beautiful, glossy, dark green, pinnate leaves that are an attractive feature year round. For months through late spring and summer, it produces its pale pink trumpet-shaped flowers, with a blood red throat, that can reach 3cm in diameter. It prefers a warm-temperate to subtropical climate and full sun, needs good drainage, and is frost tender. The best feature is its very long flowering period. There are a number of exciting cutivars of this species available and all are highly recommended. 'Lady Di' has beautiful, snow white flowers, while 'Deep Pink' is self-explanatory as is 'Lemon Bells'. 'Southern Belle' has pale pink flowers that are larger than normal and the plant has a less vigorous climbing habit, which means it can be used as a low-growing shrub provided it is pruned a couple of times a year.

Pandorea pandorana (wonga wonga vine)
This vigorous climber will grow to cover the support it is given. It has similar but smaller foliage and flowers to *Pandorea jasminoides* (listed above). The tubular flowers are 2–3cm long by 1cm wide and are usually a creamy colour with a purplish throat, although there are other colours available (see cultivars below). It produces a stunning massed display of flowers in early spring, however this only lasts a few weeks. It is an extremely fast-growing plant that will fill a bare fence in no time. The species adapts well to most soil types and a wide range of climates, and is reasonably frost tolerant. A couple of cultivars with different coloured flowers are worth growing. 'Snow Bells' has creamy white flowers borne in early spring, while 'Golden Showers' has rather spectacular, bronze-yellow flowers.

Passiflora cinnabarina (red passion flower)
This spectacular native climber is closely related to the exotic, edible passionfruit (*Passiflora edulis*). It is very vigorous and will expand to cover whatever sized support it is given. The large, dark green, lobed leaves are attractive all year round, and through spring and early summer it produces lots of intricate, bright red passion flowers. It can be cultivated on a wide range of soil types (provided the drainage is reasonable) and climates, and it is moderately frost tolerant. Prune lightly after flowering to encourage a dense bushy habit.

Persoonia species (geebungs)
The various geebungs should be considered as much for their rich mid-green foliage as for their small but attractive yellow flowers. There are about 90 species in the Australian bush, however, not many are readily available in nurseries. It is worth checking with your local native nursery.

Persoonia chamaepitys (prostrate geebung)
This outstanding geebung forms a soft carpet no more than 30cm high and it can spread to a width of more than 1m. The linear, mid-green leaves form a dense groundcover that is highlighted with masses

Phebalium 'Green Screen', an interesting new cultivar, ideal for hedging

Grass Tree (*Xanthorrhoea* species), perfect for providing interest and texture in your garden

A kaleidoscope of potted colour

The Hill's Hoist provides an intriguing but perhaps appropriate backdrop to an Australian plant garden

Imaginative pots can enhance colour effects

of fragrant, deep yellow flowers in spring. It does require good drainage and full to part sun and it will tolerate heavy frosts.

Persoonia pinifolia (pine-leaved geebung)
This is arguably the best geebung for the garden with its outstanding foliage, flowers and fruits. It will grow to 2–3m tall by several metres wide, and has attractive soft, deep green, needle-like foliage that is a feature in itself. The ends of the branches are lit up with golden yellow clusters of flowers from summer through autumn. In winter and spring, clusters of purplish grape-like fruits add to the year-round interest of this species. It requires a well-drained soil and full to part sun and it will tolerate moderate frosts. It responds well to moderate pruning and the foliage, flowers and fruits are excellent for cut-flower arrangements.

Phebalium species
This rather large genus of shrubs belongs to the citrus family (Rutaceae) and is almost exclusively Australian. Generally, the feature of the phebaliums is their masses of small starry flowers, usually yellow, cream or white, in springtime.

Phebalium 'Green Screen'
This is a very dense, vigorous hybrid between *Phebalium elatius* and *P. lamprophyllum* that grows to about 2m high and up to 2m wide, but can be kept smaller by regular pruning during the growing season. This compact shrub remains bushy at ground level, making it ideal for screening or hedging. It features bright green, aromatic foliage and the plant is covered in massed clusters of small, starry, white flowers during late winter and spring. An added bonus is the plant's ability to attract butterflies and birds to the garden. It is very hardy and grows in heavy or light soils with reasonable drainage, in full sun to shaded positions, and is hardy to moderate frosts and extended dry periods.

Phebalium squamulosum (forest phebalium)
This widespread species has many different forms and occurs in the wild from Queensland to Victoria. It is the hardiest phebalium in cultivation and the most commonly grown forms reach a height of about 2–3m by 1–2m wide. The ends of the numerous branches are smothered in masses of small, creamy yellow, star-shaped flowers in early to mid-spring, and the flowers can be cut for indoor decoration. The species adapts well to almost any soil type with reasonable drainage, requires full to part sun, and is hardy to moderate frosts. Pruning back the bush by 20 to 30 per cent after flowering will keep the plant compact and bushy.

Phebalium stenophyllum 'Golden Glow'
This is a very attractive selection of a small-growing, hardy species that forms a small rounded shrub to 1.2m high and 1m wide. It features massed, bright yellow flowers with long, fluffy stamens during late winter and spring. It suits all well-drained, acid to slightly alkaline soils, and full sun to partially shaded positions. It will withstand dry periods and moderate frosts. From a colour point of view, it is an outstanding bright yellow that can be used in the border or for container planting.

Philotheca (syn. *Eriostemon*) species and cultivars
This is another important Australian genus that belongs to the citrus family (Rutaceae). The plants bear masses of starry flowers, usually in white and sometimes mauve. Many of the plants formerly known as *Eriostemon* have now been placed into this genus by botanists. Apart from *Philotheca myoporoides* mentioned below, it is worth looking for other compact, profuse-flowering members of this genus such as *P. buxifolia* and *P. verrucosa*.

Philotheca myoporoides (syn. *Eriostemon myoporoides*) (long-leaf waxflower)
By far the hardiest of all the *Philotheca* species is the long-leaf waxflower, which can be found in a wide variety of habitats from southeastern Queensland through New South Wales and down into Victoria. Throughout this extensive range, numerous variants can be found, all of which are adaptable to cultivation. The most common forms in cultivation grow to a height and width of 2–3m. The narrow leaves can be up to 12cm in length and are aromatic. The plant is smothered in starry white flowers in early spring, and will survive drought and virtually any soil conditions provided there is reasonable drainage. It responds well to pruning of any sort. There are also several outstanding cultivars that have been selected from this species including 'Profusion', which has attractive blue-green coloured foliage that releases a fresh apple-like fragrance when brushed against. 'Stardust' is another beauty, growing to about 1.5m tall and flowering profusely. 'Bush Beauty' grows to about 50cm high by 1m wide and features massed, pink buds and white flowers from August to November.

Pimelea species and cultivars (rice flowers)

The rice flowers are an underrated group of Australian plants that have a lot to offer with a wide variety of flower colours and flowering times among the 90 or so species found in the wild. They are generally small, compact shrubs that attract butterflies when in bloom.

Pimelea ferruginea (rice flower)
This dwarf shrub (growing to 1m in height and width) with attractive, small, dark green leaves is probably the best and most popular species in cultivation. It has masses of small pink flowers, about 5cm in size, that are held in pompom clusters at the ends of the branches in spring. It needs plenty of sunshine and good drainage to perform at its spectacular best. The species tolerates coastal conditions well, is hardy to moderate frosts, and will also survive dry conditions very well. It should be lightly pruned after flowering. There are some outstanding cultivars of this species, such as 'Bonne Petite' with spectacular deep pink flowers and 'Magenta Mist' with striking cerise-pink flowers that have contrasting white centres and a flowering period that lasts for many weeks.

Pimelea linifolia (slender rice flower)
This small shrub generally grows about 1m high and wide, and has the great advantage of flowering for most of the year. The rather subtle flowers can vary from white to pink and are prominently displayed in 5cm-wide heads at the ends of the branches. The species adapts well to a wide variety of soil and climatic conditions, can thrive with less than perfect drainage, and is moderately frost tolerant. Light shade provides a similar environment to its natural habitat. Trim lightly after a major flush of flowers in order to keep the plant compact. The cultivars 'Pygmy White' and 'Snowfall' are naturally dwarfed to grow less than 50cm in height.

Pittosporum species

This group of shrubs and small trees contains some outstanding glossy-leafed plants, usually perfumed, with white flowers that are often followed by brightly coloured fruits. They are a worthy addition to the garden. Australia has about 20 species of *Pittosporum* and there are dozens of others scattered across the Southern Hemisphere, particularly in New Zealand where many of the popular hedging cultivars originate.

Pittosporum rhombifolium (hollywood, diamond laurel)
One of the rather interesting common names of this species derives from the attractive glossy leaves being diamond-shaped like those of the exotic holly plant, rather than being an allusion to the glitzy suburb of Los Angeles in the United States. While it usually forms a large shrub up to 5m high by 3m wide, it can grow to a height of 15m when crowded by other plants. It has masses of small, white, sweetly fragrant flowers in late spring and early summer that are followed by a rather spectacular display of orange-yellow fruits at the ends of the branches. It will grow equally well in full sun or light shade and requires a well-drained soil. This species and will withstand moderate frosts.

Pittosporum undulatum (sweet pittosporum)
A tall shrub or small tree that can grow to 12m high by 7m wide, this species features very attractive, glossy leaves with a distinctive wavy margin. The masses of small, creamy white flowers in spring and early summer give off a heady perfume that leads to this species sometimes being given the common name of native daphne. It is a very adaptable plant, as long as reasonable drainage is provided, and will withstand moderate frosts. It can be pruned into a hedge if desired, but it needs to be said that the species seeds readily and can become a weed and should not be planted in areas adjacent to natural bushland.

Prostanthera species and cultivars (native mint bushes)

The mint family (Lamiaceae) has many Australian representatives, a large number of which are exquisitely and strongly fragrant. The native mint bushes are the best examples, and in most cases the leaves are very aromatic and even the slightest brush against them will release their heady mint-like perfume.

Prostanthera lasianthos (Victorian Christmas bush)
A large shrub that will grow to a height of up to 8m by several metres wide, this species can be found thriving in shaded gullies on the coastal slopes in southeastern Australia. As the common name suggests, the masses of pleasantly fragrant flowers are produced at Christmas time and are whitish, pale pink or pale blue, with the inside of the flower spotted or blotched with brown or yellow. It requires good drainage, is moderately frost tolerant, and does best in light shade.

Prostanthera ovalifolia (oval-leafed mint bush)
This is the best known of the native mint bushes and grows to a height of about 3m high by about 2m wide. It is so floriferous that the mid-spring display of purple flowers usually completely obscures the leaves, giving rise to another of its common names, the thousand-flowered mint bush. It requires excellent drainage and a sheltered position with light shade, and it is a good idea to mimic nature by providing a deep organic mulch around the base of the plant. It should be pruned lightly after flowering and protected from heavy frost. It looks stunning when planted with yellow-flowering plants such as wattles and is worth the effort.

Prostanthera 'Poorinda Ballerina'
This delightful white-flowered plant forms an upright, small shrub (2m tall by 1m wide) with small, dark green, linear leaves and masses of patterned, white flowers in spring. It is reasonably frost tolerant, is very spectacular and, more importantly, very reliable in gardens from Perth to Sydney. It can be effectively used as a feature or as a screen plant.

Prostanthera rotundifolia (round-leafed mint bush)
This is a medium-sized shrub that grows to a height of 2–3m by 1m wide and is

arguably the most spectacular native mint bush when in flower. Flowering is in mid-spring, when the leaves disappear from sight while the pink, mauve, lilac or violet blooms cover the plant. It should be pruned lightly after flowering, protected from heavy frost, and given a lightly shaded position.

Rhodanthe species (paper daisies)

The paper daisies were formerly placed in the genus *Helipterum*, however a recent revision by botanists changed that name to *Rhodanthe*. Whatever the name, these plants represent a tremendous way of introducing some quick colour to a garden of Australian plants. There are both annual and perennial types of *Rhodanthe* available and all are very easy to grow, either in the garden or in containers, provided you have reasonably good drainage and plenty of sunlight.

Rhodanthe anthemoides (syn. *Helipterum anthemoides*) (chamomile sunray)
This outstanding perennial species forms a bushy shrublet to 50cm high and wide. It has small, linear, grey-green foliage that has an aroma not unlike chamomile when crushed. It has masses of small, white, everlasting, star-like flowers, which have intense red pigmentation at the base. It often flowers sporadically throughout the year, with a peak from late winter through spring. It does best in a well-drained soil in light shade and will withstand moderate frosts. Prune lightly after a flush of flowers. 'Paper Baby', 'Paper Cascade' and 'Paper Star' are all compact cultivars well worth growing.

Rhodanthe chlorocephala subsp. *rosea* (syn. *Helipterum roseum*) (rosy sunray)
This is one of Australia's outstanding annual plants for providing a splash of colour in the garden. It grows to a height of 50cm–1m by 30cm wide, and has narrow,

linear, grey-green leaves which are crowned by large papery flowers that range from very dark pink to white with yellow or black centres. Cultivation is the same as for *Rhodanthe manglesii* (listed below).

Rhodanthe manglesii (syn. *Helipterum manglesii*) (pink sunray)
A fantastic annual that grows to a height of about 50cm with a spread of about 30cm, this species features heart-shaped, greyish green leaves. Through spring and early summer, it produces masses of silvery, pendulous buds that open into delicate pink or white papery flowers. Seed is sown in autumn and can be planted directly into its final position in a well-drained soil in the garden. It is hardy to moderate frosts.

Rhododendron lochae (native rhododendron)

Australia's only native rhododendron grows to about 1m in height and width and makes a wonderful pot plant, especially in cooler climates where it can then be protected from frosts. It produces its bright red, trumpet-shaped flowers among the large, dark green, ovate leaves for an extended period in spring and summer. The plant does best when given dappled sunlight. It will tolerate temperatures as low as –3°C and should be lightly pruned after flowering.

Scaevola species and cultivars (fan flowers)

The fan flowers bring a beautiful range of blues and purples to the garden, as well as adaptability and hardiness. The distinctive flowers have five petals that are all on one side, giving a hand-like appearance. The windswept headlands from which a number of species originate are subject to high salt levels and fluctuating soil moisture levels. It is no surprise, therefore, that these plants thrive when provided with favourable conditions in pots or garden beds. Flower colours vary from white to pink through various shades of mauve, purple and blue and the plants have very long flowering periods, often from spring through to autumn. So the fan flowers can be added to the garden to provide highlights throughout the warmer months. They also make superb specimens for container growing.

Scaevola albida

This is a compact groundcover that can spread to a diameter of 1m or so. The small, dark green leaves form a dense mat that is covered for much of the year in small white, pink or blue fan-shaped flowers. The species will do well in a wide range of soils provided the drainage is reasonable and it will flower best in full sun or light shade. It will also tolerate moderate frosts.

Scaevola hookeri

This is a groundcover that spreads to a diameter of about 50cm and bears small white flowers during spring and summer. The species thrives in damp soils and full sun or light shade and is also tolerant of heavy frosts.

Scaevola 'Mauve Clusters'

The dark mauve flower colour distinguishes this groundcover, which grows up to 1m or more in diameter with small, oval-shaped leaves that are slightly lobed. The fan-shaped flowers are about 1.5cm in size, dark mauve in colour, and the plant will flower sporadically throughout the year and in profusion in spring and summer. It requires well-drained soil and will grow equally well in full sun or semi-shade. A light trim after flowering will help to keep the plant looking its best.

Scaevola 'Purple Fanfare'

This cultivar is very similar to 'Mauve Clusters' (listed above) except that it has beautiful purple flowers.

Scaevola 'Super Clusters'

This fast growing, dense groundcover reaches a height of about 30cm and a spread of about 2m, and is a new release from Merricks Nursery in Victoria. It features masses of vibrant mauve flowers throughout the year, peaking during the warmer months. Its prolific flowering makes 'Super Clusters' a great choice for border planting, embankments, rockeries, groundcover and containers.

Sollya heterophylla (bluebell creeper)

This vigorous twining creeper will rapidly cover whatever support it is given in the garden, be it a fence, stump or whatever. The medium-sized leaves are up to 5cm long and are interspersed with small, blue, bell-shaped flowers throughout spring and summer. It is very adaptable to different soil types and hardy to most frosts, and will perform in full sun to moderate shade. It makes an excellent screen plant and is one of our few blue-flowered creepers.

Stenocarpus sinuatus (firewheel tree)

This spectacular tree belongs to the protea family (Proteaceae) and can grow to a height of 20m with a width of about 5–10m. The glossy, dark green, 12cm-long, lobed leaves are a feature in themselves and in late summer and autumn they become a worthy backdrop for the fiery red flower heads that are each about 7–10cm in diameter. The flowers are also magnets for birds, making this an excellent feature tree for larger gardens. It requires a deep, well-drained soil and full sun, and will tolerate light frosts.

Swainsona formosa (syn. *Clianthus formosus*) (Sturt's desert pea)

This is a spectacular groundcovering or trailing plant that is best grown as an annual to provide a spectacular spring display. It has greyish green, pinnate leaves that are attractive in their own right and spectacular clusters of red, pea-shaped flowers that have a distinctive black centre. Being a desert plant, it requires dry conditions and is best grown in a pot if you don't have good drainage in your garden. Water it sparingly and try and keep the foliage dry. It tolerates light frost and should be given full sunlight. It is possible to purchase grafted plants that use a much hardier plant as a rootstock thus ensuring a longer life for your plant. As a trailing plant, it makes a great rockery specimen and is also a good plant to cover a wall.

Syzygium species and cultivars (lillypillies)

The common name lillypilly is applied to a number of plants in the genera *Syzygium* and *Acmena*. The common feature is their dense, glossy green foliage, fluffy creamy white flowers, and colourful fleshy fruits that can be white to various shades of pink and red. All the lillypillies can be pruned into whatever shape you desire, the pruning also stimulating the colourful new growth in the warmer months of the year.

Syzygium australe (scrub cherry)
This is an evergreen shrub or small tree, up to 8m in height by 5m wide, with creamy-coloured summer flowers followed by bright red edible fruits. It does best in full to part sun, requires good drainage, and is frost tender. 'Blaze' is a compact form about 4–5m in height, with the outstanding feature being the fiery red new growth that occurs throughout the warmer months. 'Minipilly' has a height and width of about 2m with bronze-coloured new growth and pink fruits. 'Bush Christmas' has orange new growth and grows to 2–3m high by 1.5m wide. 'Tiny Trev' has the smallest leaves of this group of cultivars, being just 2–3cm long. The plant grows into a conical form about 1m in height without any pruning whatsoever.

Syzygium paniculatum (brush cherry)
The wild form of this species is a tree that can grow to 20m high by 8m wide; however, there are also several dwarf, shrubby cultivars (listed below). The white flowers are borne in summer and are followed by edible crimson fruits. The leaves can be up to 8cm long and ovate in shape, with bronze-red new growth which is a feature in itself. It requires full to part sun and good drainage and is somewhat frost tender. 'Lilliput' is a dwarf form that grows to about 2m in height and width, and tends to assume a compact, bun shape even without pruning. 'Little Lil' grows to 1–1.5m in height and width and is fast growing. 'Elite' grows into a large shrub about 4–5m in height and about 2m in width and has very attractive, pinkish new growth.

Telopea species and cultivars (waratahs)

The waratahs are a spectacular group for bringing fiery red tones into your garden. The key to unlocking their potential lies in understanding their growing requirements: a deep, well-drained soil, plenty of light, and the right quantity and balance of nutrients throughout the warmer months. Use a low-phosphorus fertiliser recommended for natives—a couple of handfuls at the beginning of spring and then again in mid- to late summer. Prune back the plants by one-third after flowering has finished or cut the flowers for arrangements, pruning the plant in the process.

Telopea 'Shady Lady'
This hybrid between the New South Wales waratah and the Gippsland waratah (*Telopea oreades*) forms a medium-sized to large shrub that grows 2–5m tall by 2–3m wide. The leaves are dark green, large and spoon shaped with a smooth margin. The flower heads are showy but not as large as those of the New South Wales waratah and do not have the

large red bracts that are also such a feature in the New South Wales waratah. It flowers in late spring and sometimes in autumn as an added bonus. It performs well in light shade but the name can be a bit misleading, as it will not flower well in deep shade.

Telopea speciosissima (New South Wales waratah)
The typical form of this species grows to a medium shrub, up to 5m tall by about 4–5m wide. It has large, leathery, mid-green leaves that have prominent serrated margins. The species is moderately frost hardy. 'Wirrimbirra White' has pure white flowers in early to mid-spring. 'Olympic Flame' has bright red flowers with very large, showy bracts which surround and highlight the flower head. 'Fire and Brimstone' features brilliant red flowers, while 'In The Pink' has soft pink blooms.

Themeda triandra (kangaroo grass)

This is an attractive and versatile low-growing Australian native grass, about 50cm tall and wide. Leaf colour varies from light green to blue (see 'Mingo' below) and this can be a real feature in itself. The wiry, dark brown flower heads also add an interesting colour and texture to your garden. The plants need little or no maintenance apart from removing spent leaves and flower heads. The plant is at home in most soils, and is drought and frost tolerant. 'Mingo' is a lovely new cultivar featuring soft, blue, strap-like foliage. It is an ideal plant for rockeries, as a low border, for planting on sloping sites, and as a low groundcover under trees and shrubs or in open sunny positions.

Thryptomene saxicola 'Payne's Hybrid'

This absolutely outstanding cultivar is a must-have for the colourful native garden. It is a member of the myrtle family (Myrtaceae), and has proved itself to be extremely reliable and long lived in cultivation. It grows into a dense shrub about 1m high and wide and is smothered in small, cup-shaped, pink flowers in spring with sprinkles of flowers virtually throughout the year—for this reason alone, it is highly recommended. It is also reasonably frost resistant and tolerates less than perfect drainage. For the best flowering performance, give the plant as much sun as possible.

Thysanotus multiflorus (fringe lily)

The fringe lily adds a lovely colour to the garden. The soft, mauve flowers have delicately fringed petals and, while each flower only opens for one day at a time, there are numerous flowers produced over a long period in the spring. The fringe lily is an ideal plant for rockeries or pot culture as it grows to no more than 40cm upwards and outwards. It requires full sun or light shade. It can be fed with any complete fertiliser towards the end of winter. Cut back the old flower stems as low as possible to the ground after flowering has finished.

Trachymene caerulea (Rottnest Island daisy)

The Rottnest Island daisy is not a true daisy and actually belongs to the carrot and celery family (Apiaceae). It is widely grown overseas as a cut flower where it is known as blue lace, a very good name for the delicate terminal flower heads. The plant itself is an annual that can be sown directly into its final position in the garden and it grows to a height of 1m or so. As with many other annuals, it is a good idea to pinch out the shoot tips when the plants are 5–10cm high to encourage lots of branches and therefore lots more flowers. This plant will grow in most situations and should be given as much sunlight as possible.

Verticordia species (feather flowers)

It is hard to imagine a more colourful and spectacular genus than the exclusively Western Australian feather flowers. They come in a huge range of bright, eye-catching flower colours and the flowers appear in spring. However, it is hard to get too excited about them for the average garden as they have proved to be unreliable over a wide range of conditions over the years. But, for the enthusiast, they are well worth trying in pots: *Verticordia grandis* (scarlet feather flower) and *V. plumosa* (mauve feather flower) are the pick of the bunch. Give them perfect drainage, full sun and a frost-free position and water them sparingly for best results.

Viola hederacea (native violet)

The native violet (*Viola hederacea*), with its masses of purple and white flowers, has deservedly become very popular with all sorts of gardeners. Its small, rounded leaves form a thick carpet about 20cm high that smothers most weed competition and the plants are rarely, if ever, without flowers. It is an extremely adaptable plant that will tolerate heavy frost and poorly drained moist soils, and it flowers well even in deep shade. It is also very easy to propagate and can be multiplied very quickly by simply dividing young plantlets from the parent plant and putting them straight back into soil to establish.

Wahlenbergia species and cultivars

The Australian bluebells (*Wahlenbergia* species) belong to the family Campanulaceae, which contains such well-known plants as Canterbury bells (*Campanula medium*). While the Australian bluebells do not have the large, spectacular flowers of the Northern Hemisphere types, they do have lots of small, dainty blue flowers that add a beautiful touch to any garden.

Wahlenbergia gloriosa (Australian bluebell) This perennial grows to a height of 30–40cm and can spread up to 1m wide. Plant it at the edge of a garden bed or rockery or in a large container. It has large, dark blue flowers, 3cm in size, throughout late spring and summer. It requires full sun or part shade and well-drained soil, and is very frost tolerant.

Westringia fruticosa (coast rosemary)

The greyish green foliage of this hardy shrub that grows 2m tall by 3m wide makes it an outstanding background plant for all sorts of other plants. The leaves are small and lanceolate and are decorated with small white flowers for most of the year. This plant will perform well in full sun to part shade, will tolerate virtually any soil conditions, and is indestructible even under coastal conditions. It can also be pruned into a hedge or screen of any shape, and is frost tolerant.

Xanthorrhoea species (grass trees)

The grass trees are a bold and dramatic addition to any garden. In the wild, they usually have a jet black trunk, as a result of bushfire, contrasting with a splash of beautiful, cascading, linear green leaves. There are many different species of grass tree throughout Australia so it is best to enquire at your nursery as to what is locally available. All grass trees are able to grow well in either full sun or light shade and most will withstand moderate frosts. Grass trees adapt well to a range of soil types, even ones where drainage is not good. It is advisable to apply a low-phosphorus native plant fertiliser in springtime and it should also be said that grass trees are naturally slow-growing plants.

Obtaining unusual Australian plants

It is often very difficult to find some of the rarer Australian plants in regular garden centres. There are, of course, specialist native plant nurseries in every State. One of the best, and which also offers an Australia-wide freighting service, is:

Kuranga Native Nursery
393 Maroondah Highway
Ringwood
Victoria
Phone 03 9879 4076
Fax 03 9870 7301

The Australian Plant Society is a wonderful way to learn more about Australian plants and contact details can be found in the capital city phone book for each State.

Index of plant (botanic) names

Index of plant (common) names